ABOUT TH

Stafford Whiteaker, who was a member of a Christian monastic community, has a degree in Psychology and Language, as well as training in Group Psychotherapy. The author of the highly successful *The Little Book of Inner Space*, as well as Europe's bestselling book on spiritual retreats, *The Good Retreat Guide*, he writes and broadcasts regularly on spiritual matters. He lives in a farming village in France.

LIVING THE SACRED

SACRED

Ten Gateways to Open Your Heart

STAFFORD WHITEAKER

RIDER
LONDON · SYDNEY · AUCKLAND · JOHANNESBURG

Acknowledgements

With thanks to my brothers and sisters at Turvey Abbey and Annie Sachs-Marie for loving support and for places to write.

1 3 5 7 9 10 8 6 4 2

First published in 2000 by Rider,
an imprint of Ebury Press, Random House,
20 Vauxhall Bridge Road, London SW1V 2SA
www.randomhouse.co.uk

Random House Australia (Pty) Limited
20 Alfred Street, Milsons Point, Sydney,
New South Wales 2061, Australia

Random House New Zealand Limited
18 Poland Road, Glenfield,
Auckland 10, New Zealand

Random House South Africa (Pty) Limited
Endulini, 5A Jubilee Road,
Parktown 2193, South Africa

The Random House Group Limited Reg. No. 954009

Acknowledgement is made to HarperSanFrancisco for quotation of the poem, 'What Jesus Runs Away From' from *The Essential Rumi*, translated by Coleman Barks (copyright © 1995) and to The Islamic Texts Society for quotation from *al-Ghazali: Invocations and Supplications*, Book IX (copyright © 1990).

Papers used by Rider are natural, recyclable products made from wood grown in sustainable forests.

Printed and bound in Great Britain by Biddles of Guildford

A CIP catalogue record for this book is available from the British Library

ISBN 0 7126 0894 X

CONTENTS

Sing out my soul.
Arise incense of prayer.
Make these none other
Than gates to Heaven.

9th-century hymn

THE GARDEN OF THE SOUL

H ere is what you need to know about living a sacred life: it does not matter who you are or what your age. Never mind your religion or lack of it. No matter that you do not even whisper the name of God in your mind. A life so far spent in disbelief is less than a drop of water in the ocean of your spiritual realm. Do not fear if your mind or body is weak. Have no concern for your poverty or wealth. None of these matter.

You have a spirit and that spirit lives within you. It connects you with everyone else and makes you one with Creation itself. You are not alone in this life for you belong to everything on earth and in the universe from the ladybird in your garden to the stars beyond the sun. And everything also belongs to you. The holiness that holds all this together is a mystery which we may call God. This eternal unknown lives within you because you are of God, as is all life and matter in the cosmos. Since God has no beginning nor ending and you exist in God, you too have neither beginning nor ending. This vision of the eternal makes the soul hope.

The golden need of the heart

Our longing for peace and our desire to get away from it all testify to our need for the time and space to be our true selves. These moments of interior calm, when we manage to get them, can bring a feeling of unity. It is then that a sense of the sacred in our lives usually arises. This invisible thing, this hidden aspect of self calls to us and we recognise it as a deep yearning for answers to profound questions – Who am I? What am I? What is the meaning of my life? This voice that calls is the soul.

The soul is like a secret garden hidden deep within us. The flowers of love bloom there, fragrant with our sweetest hopes. Mysterious and beckoning, it is the place of myths and dreams, the home of our spirit. We cannot define it. We often forget it. Yet we long to dwell there. It gives birth to our senses of wonder and belonging. It is where we seek the truths and meanings about ourselves which science cannot give us. Like the wind that stirs the stilled leaf, the soul awakens in us a movement towards the eternal. This garden of the soul knows no time or space. It is as intimate and immediate as your fingers touching your lips and as vast as the cosmos which has no beginning or ending.

To neglect the soul denies the spiritual dimension of life. It means we are restricted by the limitations of our bodies and minds – no matter how wonderful these may be. Without the leadership of the spirit to give us a moral basis for living and a deeper vision of self than the ego can provide, we become ruled by our ever changing desires and notoriously unreliable senses. These are great hindrances to knowing God.

In seeking the garden of our soul, in searching for the sacred, we free our spirit and begin to unite our body, mind and spirit. In this way we can begin to be one with all Creation. We put an end to our useless sense of possession and become aware that we belong to the myriad creatures that share this planet, to the moon and stars and to the very stones at our feet. We realise that our life is not separate but a continuous part of all visible and invisible nature. Such transformation is to be found only in the realm of the inner self where the soul waits to be discovered.

Imagine for a moment the garden of your soul. It is surrounded by a great wall built up by your sense of self-importance. Your ego stands guard, hoping to bar your way. But here and there are ancient gateways into the garden. They have existed perhaps since humans first gazed up at the heavens and they are to be found in one form or another in all the great spiritual traditions of the world. When you go through one of them, you begin to live a sacred life.

There is the Gateway of Stillness, a direct step into inner space where you may find rest in that silence and solitude which gives repose to your spirit and health to your body. When worries fill you up and relationships fail, the Gateway of Mindfulness leads you back to being present in the moment so you can regain perspective and grasp true realities. It helps you recognise illusion, the source of human suffering. If you would hear with your heart, then you must enter the Gateway of Listening, where there are voices which speak of your true self. The Gateway of Meditation frees the spirit, refuses entry to worldly desires and concerns and calms the mind. The Gateway of Loving leads to a life of compassion which makes you desire only the will of God. Then the soul cries out: 'Oh, God, I am yours! Come, Beloved!'

The moments when we are conscious of the splendour of the world around us are manifold. When you watch an ant or when your eye catches the shining colour of a dragonfly, you may feel awe at such marvellous works of efficiency and beauty. When you hear lightning and thunder, you may become a child afraid of the overwhelming unknown. When you wake in the arms of your beloved, you may feel blissful peace. When the colours of autumn fill you with awe, your heart fills with joy. In such moments you are fully alive in life and this is the mark of your awareness of Creation itself. This fosters a unity with the eternal and the

Gateway of Celebration opens wide and raises the soul up in songs of praise for this divine union.

The Gateway of Dreaming leads to a rediscovery of innocence that restores hope. Without dreams, hope fades and the vision of the soul grows faint. The Gateway of Affirmation is decorated with the blessings in your life and lets you take stock of the way you are presently living. If you would talk with God, then the Gateway of Prayer is the way of the pure heart. The Gateway of Creativity brings into existence your hidden gifts and helps you live a life of spiritual values.

The holy realm of Wisdom is to be found when you pass through these ancient and holy gateways to the soul. Here hidden realities become visible and the self is grounded in truth. Wisdom is the Crown of God and she will bring you an understanding of the meaning of your life.

The jewel within the heart

Rich or poor, powerful in this world or not, you can open your heart to richness of the spirit. The hope of Paradise lies within us because we are human. It is the jewel of our nature. To deny yourself awareness of this yearning is to keep self-knowledge hidden. How can we ever hope to know ourselves if we deny such a defining element of our humanity? We are made as much by myth and symbol as we are by physical fact, existing in a perplexing state where conscious realities are illuminated by the rising and falling of our hidden ones. Our manifestations of love for the invisible holy that lies within us and which we may chose to call *God* is dependent on no one else, nor on our worldly circumstances. If we cannot at least love this *idea* of the eternal, how can we claim to have love and compassion for others, which is so much more difficult?

Beneath the superficial differences between cultures and people there are underlying universals. One of these is primal experiences which are remarkably common. These fundamental spiritual experiences shatter our preconceived notions about the rational order of the universe. They are more profound than the latest discovery of science because they are intimately personal. Who can say what starts any of us on the inner journey to discover the sacred? What makes humanity so sensitive to the inner feelings of the heart? Our journey towards God often begins without a great event taking place in our life. We are going about the ordinary business of our daily living, when almost without perception, something stirs in our consciousness. The soul calls to us as it has called for millions of men and women throughout human history. Our spirit awakes and our sacred journey begins.

Because it transcends gender, race, class and culture, in a sense this journey for self-knowledge and personal enlightenment is a process that begins even before we are born. Yet the universal spiritual journey is the form of knowledge most ignored in Western education. Recent research in Britain and America confirms that most people believe there is a spiritual dimension to our humanity and that those people who actively lead a life involving spirituality are more likely to have good emotional health.

Your spiritual self exists and lives within you at this very moment, and from time to time everyone hears something that goes straight to the heart of their being. A *Newsweek* poll found that 58 per cent of people in America feel the need to experience spiritual growth and 33 per cent have had a religious or mystical experience. In a recent British survey, over 60 per cent of people said they had had some form of spiritual revelation. There is no reason why you should not be among them.

From the moment of conception we forge our individuality. In our mother's womb we move to a dance of our own preference. This insistence on self and our search for control over our destiny will define our entire life. It will influence all our important decisions. It will help or hinder us in our search for love. It will be both a blessing and a curse and we shall not be rid of it until we are dead. And then who knows? Perhaps it materialises in another realm? What is certain is that we have three dimensions to our being – the physical, the mental and the spiritual. These are not separate parts of us but intimate aspects of the same oneness. We yearn for a perfect union with our vision of what our life should be. The hard reality is that we soon discover that we are defined as much by other human beings as by what we claim to be our true identity. If we give up our vision we suffer the plagues of the inner self – depression, anger, frustration, envy, greed – all the destructive forces of a frustrated nature. Unhappiness becomes our mode of living because we are alienated from our true feelings. When we lose sight of our vision we desert our soul and turn to a life of substitution where we hope every amusement and passing pleasure of the ego will fill our inner emptiness. But these worldly values are no substitute for our intuitive sense of identity, vision and creativity. Such substitution diminishes spiritual values and fragments the self. It is the curse of our age.

Arrows from heaven:

Sacred texts that awaken your spirit

A question many people ask when they begin their spiritual pilgrimage is whether they need to belong to a particular religion or follow some idealised person or routine. Of course, it helps to go to church, synagogue or temple: these are places for the faithful of a defined spiritual way, and going to services can be very supportive and conductive to forming the habit of taking time for the spiritual. The singing and chanting, the praying together and all the initiations and rituals of religion help to release our spiritual feelings. Yet too often church is just a habit and, worst of all, uninspiring, and this does not help us to live a sacred life. However, a study of the sacred texts of the great world religions demonstrates that the same essential truths of the spiritual life are to be found in the words of all holy prophets and saints. Reading them we discover that all of us are the inheritors of the sacrifice of Christ, the transcending wisdom of the Buddha, the inspirational mystery of Krishna, and the holy obedience of Mohammed. These are pearls in the spiritual treasure of our humanity. What sane man or woman refuses an inheritance?

The words of holy prophets can be sacred arrows that come in the form of words but change within you to burning arrows that pierce your heart and shake your beliefs. They wake you up to the fact that you are a spiritual being and make you realise your heart can be touched by the idea of the divine – no matter how little conscious attention you may have previously paid to the spiritual. This can be a revelation, one that can transform your entire life.

On the nature of God

The nineteenth-century sage and saint Sri Ramakrishna said:

> God has made different religions to suit different
> aspirants, times and countries. All doctrines are only
> so many paths; but a path is by no means God
> himself. Indeed, one can reach God if one follows
> any of the paths with wholehearted devotion. You
> have no doubt heard the story of the chameleon. A
> man entered the wood and saw a chameleon on a
> tree. He reported to his friends. 'I have seen a red
> lizard.' He was firmly convinced it was nothing but
> red. Another person, after visiting the tree, said, 'I
> have seen a green lizard.' He was firmly convinced
> that it was nothing but green. But the man who
> lived under the tree said, 'What both of you have
> said is true. But fact is that the creature is sometimes

red, sometimes green, sometimes yellow, and
sometimes has no colour at all.'

(*The Gospel of Sri Rama Krishna*, quoted by Joseph
Campbell in *The Masks of God: Primitive Mythology*)

Thus, religious belief may be defined as a person's thought about
God and, since all thoughts in the universe are attributes of God,
these human thoughts are aspects in which God reveals Himself.
Pope John Paul II said that religion needs to be seen not in any
narrow or ideological sense but rather 'as the fundamental open-
ness of the human being to the mystery which lies at the heart of
all things.'

At the heart of all religion there is a restless search for the God
of all gods who transcends time, space, matter, the unknown and
the known. This is the God who is manifest in all sacred texts from
the Bible of Judaism and Christianity to the Qur'an of Islam and
the Bhagavadgita of Hinduism, and in all the oral spiritual traditions of native peoples. This is the God who is found in nature and
in the creative expressions of our humanity.

Nothing can be closer to the truth than that God has as many
meanings, names and faces as there may be stars in the heavens.
Yet God is intimately personal – a presence, the ultimate truth,
the higher knowledge, the essence of life. Using the word *God* can
focus us and help concentrate the mind. For the North American
Indian, God is the Great Spirit that is inseparable from existence
itself. The Great Spirit dwells within and without: it is timeless,
the very force of life. Our soul mirrors its existence. When we
awaken our inner life, we evoke the living God, give unlimited
flight to our spirit, and fuel our freedom to be ourselves. We are in
a different existence where there are no rules, no measure of time,
no definition of our humanity by the world's values and opinions.
We are dwelling in the Great Spirit that nourishes all life. Our
hunger for this light of being, this bread of eternal truth, this giver
of meaning to our existence can never be fully satisfied in this life,

for our hunger comes from love and love has no measure. We are visible dwellers in the invisible eternal.

Beyond the rituals of religion and the myths we individually and collectively hold which transcend every faith and belief, is the eternal – that cosmic force that appears in all life but is discerned best by our spiritual self. To acknowledge this eternal force makes us more human, not less. But the nature of this power we may call God is elusive and every person finds his or her own understanding of it, for we exist in two ways with God: in an intimate one-to-one relationship, and in perfect created harmony with all other life and matter. We are, indeed, as much a part of the stone as of the flower, for we cannot chose to which part of Creation we belong.

Perhaps what God is *not* tells us something of the nature of this universal and continuing force. In the fourteenth century an anonymous English spiritual writer and mystic wrote down what God was not, believing we could know much more about God this way. *The Cloud of Unknowing* is his most celebrated work and remains in print to this day. Here is what he had to say on the nature of the God in his writings called *An Epistle of Discretion of Stirrings*. It seems fitting to quote it as I am about to ask you in this book to start stirring up the garden of your soul.

> Silence is not God nor is speaking. Fasting is not God nor eating. Being alone is not God nor is company God nor yet any of all the other such two opposites you find in life. He is hid between them. God may not be found by any work of your body or mind or soul but only by love of your heart. He may not be known by reason nor thought. He cannot be gotten nor traced by understanding. But he may be loved and chosen with the true will of your true self. Choose God and your life is transformed into a such harmony that all you do is not divided one from the

other but united in a balance that is at the very
centre of universal truth. You will silently speak and
speak silently and all you do will be all you are
because God exists in the interleavening of all from
the structures of the cells in your body to your
dreams and the structure of the stars. The most
important way to God is to renounce whatever does
not lead to God.

You do not have to believe in God to be with God. Your intellectual acceptance of his existence does not make him real. Reason
has no part in it. God is not an exercise in metaphysics or a concept of the mind but a condition of the inner self. It is enough for
you to look around at the world and the life in it and have a sense
of wonder at its diversity and complexity and beauty. You are not
an observer, but part of that diversity, complexity and beauty:
there is a spiritual synthesis which brings a oneness to all of life,
that connects each to the whole. If you can see that your life and
all life shares in this mystical union, then you have found God.

It is enough that you should love Creation, because love itself
is God. It lives beyond the limits of your human belief or disbelief.
It exists before you and after you. In this way, time is no measure.
Space as you see it in three dimensions is not all of reality. While
no one can see the face of God, the Divine can be seen everywhere
and it is in this kind of seeing with the inner eye of the soul that
you are united with God. It is said that when you take only one step
towards God, he advances ten steps towards you. Mohammed the
Prophet said, 'The complete truth is that God is always with you.'

Talking to God

If God is everywhere all at once, how do we talk to him? In what
direction should we address our words? The great master of Sufi
doctrine, Najm al Din Kubra (1145–1221) wrote that since every-

thing exists both within the very great and the very small, it also must exist within each human. Thus, he reasoned, the entire universe and all eternity itself exist within every person and the direction we must take to find God is an inner one. 'Know that the lower soul, the Devil, and the Angel are not external to you,' he writes. 'You *are* they. So too, Earth and the Divine Throne are not located outside nor are Paradise, Hell, Life or Death. All these exist in you, as you will realise once you have accomplished the journey and become pure.' The dwelling place of God then is in our interior realm – the place of the spirit. Everyone has such a spirit which comes from God and God has given this spirit, which is the self, ears, eyes and a heart (the Qu'ran 67:23). Al Din Kubra reminds us that 'all men are in a state of blindness save those from whom God has removed the veil. That veil is not something external to them, but is indeed of them for it consists of the darkness of their individuality.'

The love and truth we seek is the fire in the hearth of being. If there is a secret to understand, it is that our life is not something we have brought to the world, but something the world has given to us. This is the only secret that God gave away.

The everlasting desire of the heart

We are all born into a tradition of religious insights and spiritual truths. While every generation reinvents its culture for its own times, we seem today to have done more that this: we have dismissed much ancestral wisdom as if only our own generation could discern eternal truths. Much of the blame for this attitude rests with Science's claim to truth and our credulity in believing that it is indeed the ultimate process for understanding humanity and the world. One major effect of this has been to separate our values for daily living from our knowledge and heritage of the sacred, and hence our struggle has increasingly been to find some new basis for the purpose and meaning of our life. We employ language in an attempt to define our humanity, to declare the perimeters of our understanding, to mark our culture and to bring clarity to our ambitions, dreams, and fears. Yet our words are loaded with values and the more we apply to our lives what science tells us, the more these values are made inconstant. This makes us uncertain what we can believe that may be lasting. It is not a satisfactory state from which to create a feeling of unity within ourselves. In the confusion our sacred heritage is forgotten and rituals and myths which human history has handed down seem invalid.

Having taken Science as the maker of our myths and found it wanting, we seem to have ceased to intuitively understand our profound need for the spiritual in our own lives and that of our communities. We have largely ceased to be seekers of the immortal God and have become consumers of anything which we think will advance our pleasure and sense of happiness. Unfortunately, contentment is not for sale.

The American dream that enough money and success delivers a well-adjusted personality, well-being and happiness is a hypothesis that fuels capitalist cultures. Many of the values modelled and encouraged by modern society suggest that this pursuit of material wealth is worthy. But every dream has its darker side and this one is no exception. Many leading investigators of human psychology consider that we experience a sense of well-being to the extent that we can freely express our inherent potential. Our need is to orientate our lives towards the experience of living, that is *being*, rather than the consumer orientation of *having*. The essence of spirituality is a concern with *being* and the discovery of the true self so that we may realise our individual gifts, talents, and capacities in the light of eternal values rather than the passing ones of the fashion of our day. This is the desire of the heart which neither science, the media nor any political and social dogma can erase. We are not defined by our successes or failures. We become our actions, we are what we do, how we act, and what goals we move our lives towards. We are our own masters in the spiritual realm and the heart never forgets it.

The mystery in your head

Your brain is a kind of neural network running on electric signals changed, modulated, and activated by chemical transmitters and receptors. Every bit of your body has a place in the map of the brain. Your eyes do not 'see', your brain does. You can think about seeing without 'seeing' anything. You can 'see' something in your imagination as well as through your eyes. People with transponders implanted in their brain tissue have learned to think their instructions on to a computer screen. Brain scanners have even shown researchers the spot in the brain where schizophrenics 'hear' tormenting voices, the place where laughter lies, the point that stimulates a sexual orgasm, the place that triggers fear. The geography of your brain is being explored and mapped in an attempt to understand this package of matter, weighing little more than a kilogram, which has a program for consciousness and an autonomous system to keep your life going. Your brain mediates your world and some evolutionary psychologists have even claimed that our brains possess a 'God module' associated with religious experience.

Is our experience of the mystical and the transcendent then only a transmission of some mass of nerve cells in the head? Is our religious impulse towards God some left-over evolutionary survival aid? Are the universal human urges of altruism and a sense of sacrifice only outward activities predicated by our basic need to survive in the social group? Rita Carter gives an overview of the research so far into what does what and where in our brains in her book, Mapping the Mind (Orion, 1999). She thinks in answer to these questions that if God exists he certainly would have pro-

vided us with some biological mechanism with which to apprehend him. The nature, architecture, realities and phantoms of the
brain and mind remain a puzzle. So while we may be able to map
out the geography of the brain, the mind itself remains a mystery
if for no other reason than this – you cannot share in anyone else's
consciousness. That is a *knowing* that remains beyond sharing.
What we can know is ourselves, and this understanding comes
when the soul gathers up the body and mind in a unity of self that
enables us to perceive our personal reality with clarity.

Regardless of race, nationality or culture, we seem to possess a
faculty that refuses to let us deny the spiritual, and an equally persistent feeling that we are somehow not just body and mind but
spirit too. It is as if during our lives our souls are always on a journey from a half-forgotten land to an eternal home. We hunger for
the unknown as if we were once part of it but then somehow
became detached and lost our connection to it. Some might say
we long for the lost Garden of Eden.

Scientists may one day understand the true chemistry of our
happiness, desire, love, rage, and all the other aspects of humanity. They may even understand the source of our spiritual life.
Then someone is bound to put the cat among the pigeons by asking: 'But how how does it feel to be conscious? What is it like to
be dead?' So, religion as a manifestion of our spiritual impulses is
unlikely to be vanquished by scientific achievements. The scien-
tist-priest Pierre Teilhard de Chardin summed it up this way:
'Nothing in the world around us is more obvious than the existence – indeed, the *fact* – of life: and nevertheless nothing is more
elusive, more difficult to pin down, than this same life when we
try to handle it by the general methods of science.' (*The
Phenomenon of Man*). Indeed, you do not need science to revali-
date what you have found valid for your life.

Why the spiritual is important today

Do you suffer from playing too many roles and having to constantly and consciously compartmentalise your life? You may have developed the new disease called the *schizophrenia of compartmentalisation* – meaning the act of dividing into separate sections. In 1923 the biologist Julian Huxley in his *Uniqueness of Man* compared our human ability to think and act in a unified way with the much more rigid compartmentalisation of mind and behaviour in animals. Are you becoming less human? Recently the *New York Observer* used the term *compartmentalisation chic* to define people busy juggling busy schedules. Is a lifestyle of fragmentation really progress?

We are overwhelmed with information and regimes to educate our minds and improve our bodies. We demand ever closer personal relationships that bring enormous emotional pressure. We long for a sense of space. We have scant time for reflection. Yet the spiritual dimension within each of us gives us the opportunity to balance our lives, put things into perspective, and find inner peace. Medical research shows this actively contributes to our emotional well-being. An active spirituality is healing and life enhancing. Living the sacred is *good* for you.

Stress: the enemy of personal calm

Many of the challenges we meet in ordinary living are just that – the challenges of life as we know it. Illness, pain, the loss of a love, getting fired or being made redundant, not achieving the goal we had set our hearts on – all these are the hurdles of daily life. So some stress is the currency of living itself, but for millions of people it increasingly means a state of constant anxiety which can lead to poor health, difficult relationships, and emotional fragmentation.

The common values of our culture can cause daily distress which slowly eats away at any sense of calm and happiness we might have. For example, faster and faster target deadlines which confuse our sense of priority, or the increasing number of demands on us which push and pull our loyalties in several directions at once. Unemployed or not, we exist in a competitive society in which most of us can barely adjust to local market forces, never mind international or global ones. So much is beyond our control that we can feel helpless and tossed about by life as if we were a bottle adrift on the sea – but we have a message inside which reads: 'I belong to God. If found, please return me.'

The relationships we have always involve the potential for stress, but other people are not nearly as threatening to our peace of mind as the tensions that swell up and dominate our interior selves. These are created both by external values in our culture and by our internal values that demand certain standards of behaviour of ourselves. Just think about these: our ambitions, our competitiveness, our fears of failure, our relationship to our self-image, to our food, and to criticism from other people. Our goals are often unrealistic and do not reflect what, deep in our hearts, we want for our lives.

We are caught up in this collection of tensions, forces and desires, and so we succumb frequently to stress in one form or the other. The outwards signs are there: impatience with ourselves and others; lots of anger just waiting to get out; a feeling that other people do not care about us. In the end nothing seems to suit us, and nothing rewards us, and nothing brings us a sense of peace. We are whirling in a dance of stress to a tune that is composed jointly by ourselves and the society in which we live. Disappointments and failures are normal life events. We may not be able to control them but we can learn how to meet them face on, understand them, and find peace with their existence in our lives.

Stress is an arch-enemy of your spiritual life, for it blocks you from entering into your inner space. Many millions suffering from stress fail to recognise the symptoms. They think they are simply 'worried' and that they should exert more 'control' over themselves. None of us can see exactly how excessive stress enters our lives, but once we recognise it, we can start to deal with it. Many causes may be out of our control, but learning to go through one of the Gateways into the garden of the soul is a way out of the frustrations of the stress maze.

Quick stress check-up

1. Do you have difficulty sleeping?

2. Do you have frequent headaches?

3. Do you have frequent neck pain?

4. Do you experience repetitive or obsessive thinking which you cannot stop?

5. Do you over react to small challenges?

6. Do you have feelings of anxiety or a sense of being overwhelmed?

7. Are you over eating or over indulging in alcohol or sweet things like chocolate?

8. Do you always feel discontent? Uneasy? Full of tension?

Getting down to it

Although many self-help books and courses and much scientific and psychological information may prove helpful in learning about the nature of being human, nothing takes the place of actually putting things into practise. Wanting to lose weight is no good if you don't actually stop lifting that spoon up to your mouth. Thinking about a shower does not make you wet. Saving money won't happen until you stop using your credit cards and chequebook. Learning a foreign language is impossible if you do not open your mouth and speak. The same sort of thing is true of your spiritual life. Reading about spirituality is not living in the spirit. Going to church every Sunday may not bring God any closer. Continually changing from one spirituality to another, or even from religion to another, does not advance the intention of the soul, which is to make you whole and holy.

As Sufi tradition says: 'The sight of someone eating will not appease your hunger. The spiritual experiences of others cannot satisfy your yearning.' If you are to recognise your spiritual nature and bring it into your ordinary consciousness, you must *do* something – you must begin the practise of the sacred. This is the hard part, for while it is easy to understand how your fingernails grow or the effects of stress on your body, and a whole multitude of other little and big aspects of your humanity, your true self is much more mysterious. It is like God – invisible and unknown but as intimately part of you as your very cells. We need ways to self-discovery that will give us the kind of wisdom that we can use in our daily life. We need to admit to our spiritual feelings and to the importance of the holy in our lives. The revelations of self-knowledge come to us in bits and pieces and in many ways. The reading of sacred texts helps many people. An unexplained moment in nature which reveals truths helps others. The faces of God, like the names, are many.

When the eternal speaks to us it is a one-to-one conversation that can take place anywhere and at any time. Spiritual experience is widely reported by people around the world. Since religious observance as an integral part of daily life continues to decline in Europe and other large areas of the world, it is clear that our spiritual life does not depend upon going to church, synagogue, mosque or temple. Indeed, to cultivate an experience of the sacred we do not even need to believe in some supernatural deity – for example, Methodists recently debated whether to let people join their church without believing in God.

Our spiritual experiences are the unveilings of the soul, the sudden removal of those clouds hiding the unknown part of us. We become conscious of the eternal, and of belonging to all Creation. This can bring a sense of unity, love and morality into our lives. What matters is how we act on such revelations. You can choose to make all of your life a living-out of the sacred. Is this not worth wanting? Such a life can bring you a measure for your desires and illusions and give you a vision of your true self that will lift you from any poverty and make you more wealthy than all the world's riches. Is this too not worth wanting? Our very yearning for transcendent experience tells us that to practise an awareness of the spiritual must be a way to harmony in life.

No promises, only beginnings

This book is not a manual which if carefully followed will automatically enable you to jump up with joy and exclaim: 'Yippee! I have found God!' It is rather a spiritual guide for beginners – and we are all beginners in this life in knowing our true self and the invisible God. It is intended to inspire and help you to open the great gateways to the soul so your spirit is free to become part of your ordinary daily life. Then the adventure of life is not just limited to the mind and body but is liberated by the spirit into endless realms of being. The gateways enable you to pass from the desires of this world to a discovery of more lasting values that reduce the fragmentation of the self, bring meaning and unity into your life and transform ordinary days into deeply meaningful ones.

If you depend upon your own senses alone in this journey, without the mediation of spiritual wisdom, you court unhappiness and will have none of the strength that arises from a moral imperative. Ignoring sacred texts and the divine visions of the mystics is to discard your spiritual heritage. There are many visionaries, mystics and sages whose wisdom you can consult for help in your spiritual direction and development. Whether they are Zen or

Sufi masters, Christian saints, or masters from other spiritual traditions, all will have arrived at more or less the same point, which is a merging of self into the eternal Godhead of the universe. Mystics have been called the ultimate nomads of the soul, for they have gone the furthest in the unexplored regions of intimacy with God. They are map-makers of an invisible world and our guides to an interior life.

In this book I have drawn from only a few such people to inspire you or to illustrate a point in your practise of the sacred. They range from Christians like Brother Lawerence of the Resurrection and Mechthild of Magdeburg, through al Ghazali and Najim al Din Kubra of the Sufi tradition to Native Americans such as Black Elk of the Oglala Sioux. They and others continue to be wise guides to practising the sacred and in reassuring and encouraging us to believe that a personal relationship with God is possible and that the transcendent is a heritage we all share.

But the ordinary people who come and go in our lives also have much to teach us. Once I was staying as the only retreat visitor in a monastery guest house when a tramp arrived. He was old, messy, talkative, and at odds it seemed with all the world. He was put in a room down the hall from me for a night's stay in the warm. Busy at my desk, I did not especially welcome his knock at the door. When he asked to borrow a large sheet of paper I was glad to give it. After a little while there came another knock. This time he wanted a pencil. Then another knock and a request for a coloured pencil. By this time I was getting irritated because I wanted some peace in which to pray. I decided if he disturbed me again, I would tell him off. An hour passed and I was talking to God and feeling really good about myself. Then there came another knock at the door. I pulled open the door. 'Now what is it?' I demanded angrily. 'I done this for you', he said, handing me back my paper and pencils and walking away. I held the paper up. Written out with care in the simple lettering of a schoolchild were the words of the Lord's Prayer. When I returned to my prayers I meditated upon the meaning of love and upon my pride and I thanked God for this brother down the hall.

The three concepts for living the Sacred

There are three basic concepts for living the sacred. First and foremost is that there is one God. This is the cry of Abraham and the holy prophets. This is the cry of Mohammed: 'There is no God but Allah!' Many Christians and others think this belief in one God is only Christian, Jewish, or Islamic, but they would be mistaken. For example, Akhenaten, Pharaoh of Egypt fourteen centuries before Christ, declared this same truth. The concept of one God establishes the truth of the universal unity of all life and matter. That cry 'There is no God but Allah!' means that all is one, and because all is one, we are affected by everything that takes place without and within ourselves.

When you live a more spiritual life, a moment comes when the eternal power of Creation becomes personal to you. God is no longer something *out there* but something in you and with you. We know the force of Creation is still vast and grand, but somehow it has also become intimate. This is the second concept for living the sacred. When it happens it is a great event in the life of the soul, because such a deep consciousness of the eternal has lifted another veil from the mystery of our being. We have taken into our hearts a real awareness that there is one God. When this happens to us, we have acknowledged the very definition which God gave himself: 'I am who I am ... This is my name forever.' (Exodus 3:14, 15). We have proclaimed the relationship between our spirit and the eternal *I am* and willingly returned our hearts to the Godhead, the source of all oneness.

The third concept is to know God in the first person, the *I am*. When St Térèse of Lisieux (1873–1897) told God in her prayers, 'I am Térèse of Jesus', a voice came back to her saying, 'I am Jesus of Térèse'. Only when we become conscious of God in this deeply intimate way can we hope to grasp the real nature of our life. We will be reborn in the spirit. Our soul will be unchained and that which is invisible and which seems so improbable will be understood, for what our senses and mind cannot comprehend, our spirit can behold. This understanding or vision is absolute and upon it all spiritual faith is built. Our hidden true self, the *atman*, alone knows God.

The purpose of this book then is to move you forward in your search for this vision. It is a means of purifying and awakening the spirit. You will not find a *final* answer to anything. What are presented are classic gateways to the garden of your soul where you may become this *atman* who knows the holy, the Lover who looks at himself as a mirror for seeing his Beloved and looks at his Beloved as a mirror for knowing himself. In practising the sacred you hope for a direct perception of self freed of all illusions: your consciousness is cosmic; it includes all and nothing; you are in communion with the universal through the spirit alone. This is called enlightenment.

THE FIRST
GATEWAY

Stillness – The way of connecting to the Sacred

To create in yourself a state of inner calm is to take a giant step forward in living the sacred, because it stills your mind and body and lessens your sense of fragmentation. Even in the midst of a busy life you can enter the Gateway of Stillness, a path to this peacefulness which connects you to the sacred. It will give you the serenity to be able to reflect on your life, get things into perspective, and just have time to be yourself. This gives your spirit a golden chance to flourish. The use of silence is an ancient spiritual practise for achieving this interior stillness. This is why monasteries, temples and other holy places are usually hushed and undisturbed by noise, talking and people rushing about. Using the Gateway of Stillness, you can make such an oasis of peace for yourself wherever you are.

'Be quiet!' and 'Shut up!' must be among the most frequent orders given by any mother to her child, but running, shouting, crying, laughing and even screaming are a natural part of a healthy childhood. So when we think of children the last thing we might remember is their silence. But silence is also a normal part of every child, as it is of every adult, because being silent fulfills the special need we have to be still so the inner self in all its uniqueness and creativity may speak.

Silence today is more precious than gold. When was the last time you were aware of real peacefulness? No cars or the sound of traffic. No TV, radio, music, telephones ringing, or chattering friends. Ten minutes free from the endless flow of information assailing your brain. If you think the present world is overrun with the pressure and conflict of too many people, just imagine what it will be like twenty years from now. This is why we need to prepare ourselves with a strong spiritual constitution which can help us to cope with such a demanding environment. As the world becomes a global urban community and the differences between cultures fade, silence and stillness will become rare and precious commodities. They will be the most sought-after environment, superseding even the attractions of nature in their ability to refresh the human spirit and reaffirm that our humanity is more than the sum of our own discoveries and inventions.

Noise: a killer riding the air

Noise is not just something that interferes with a spiritual life. Research shows that exposure for long periods to quite low levels of noise can cause physical and psychological problems even though this noise may not hurt normal hearing. Factory workers have been found to suffer high blood pressure, putting them at cardio-vascular risk, because of persistent noise levels in their workplace. As you might imagine, children are the most affected. It has been found that children who live in urban areas with high noise levels are more likely to have difficulty in learning to read because they find it harder to recognise and understand human speech. It is thought that such children simply filter out as much sound as they can, and often that sound is from people talking.

Comparing children living in suburban areas to those living near Munich Airport, researchers found these 'airport children' had raised blood pressure and higher than normal levels of adrenaline, a stress hormone. When the airport was closed, these blood pressure and stress levels recovered to within normal ranges. What is the adult health of children who live with too high a level of noise during the whole of their childhood? What was the noise environment of your childhood? Could you be a kind of 'airport child' and now need the nourishment of silence?

You do not have to live near an airport to experience damaging background noise. Raised blood pressure and other stress symptoms can occur at sound levels of about 60 decibels. An OECD report estimated that 16 per cent of Europeans sleep with more than 40 decibels in their bedroom. The key question seems to be this: when does sound become noise and affect us? Research has not yet given final answers, but most of us would agree that while we might delight in the sound of waves on the seashore or the crackling of a hearth fire, we are unlikely to equally enjoy the sound of motorway traffic. If you suffer from depression, sounds which would not normally irritate you may well become intolerable because of your emotional state. Hospitals try to keep wards quiet because it is more restful for patients. Sleep and stillness need silence to achieve their healing effects.

Unless you live in a very remote place, you will not avoid some background sound of traffic and other noises of modern life. If you think you live in such peaceful bliss, try the test on page 34. Even a cloistered nun who accepted this challenge failed it after just two minutes when someone in the kitchen dropped a saucepan. While we cannot control public noise, our domestic lives give us some choices. We do not need to turn on the radio. We can disconnect the telephone and shut off the pager. We do not need background music and the TV is not a substitute for companionship. If you find a constant background of sound necessary, ask yourself why?

Noise test

Listen carefully for the next four minutes. Can you hear

1. Traffic?

2. People talking?

3. Television?

4. Radio?

5. Building works?

6. Dogs barking?

7. Police or fire vehicle sirens?

8. Car or other anti-theft alarms?

9. Music playing?

10. Telephone or pager calling?

If you answer *yes* to any of these you are not in a silent environment. If you answer yes to more than three questions, you may be suffering from too much noise.

There is sound wherever we go – supermarkets, restaurants, cafés, lifts, waiting rooms of every kind, train stations, airports – the list is a long one. It seems we must have auditory entertainment from the moment we wake up to our radio alarm. There is TV and world news for breakfast and car radios and personal stereos to accompany us on the way to work. Few workplaces offer silence. If the equipment we use is not very noisy then we always seem to find a reason for chatting. The length of discussions at business meetings can seem endless. Of course, we have a need to communicate and, being the sociable creatures we are, the sounds around us can reassure and give comfort. But when sound overwhelms us as it tends to do in modern life, it can bring a sense of fragmentation and cause physical and psychic distress. The soul does not like this.

Sound has a twin called Information Overload and together

they form a formidable enemy to human health and happiness. Cyber-stress is the newest feature of human life, the result of the tidal wave of information coming at us. Many people are drowning in e-mails, faxes and pager messages. The symptoms are headaches, sneezing, high blood pressure, unexplained aches and pains, and shivering. In many occupations they have reached epidemic proportions. An average office worker is now said to receive dozens of e-mail messages a day, and there are some 800 million items of unsolicited mail arriving at British businesses every year. When you look up a word on the Web, you might find over 18,000 references to it. The consequences of information overload are cumulative and could be devastating. Professor Eric Harth of Syracuse University, New York believes that we may find ourselves swamped by our own technology, which constantly grows while the intelligence we need to handle and survive it may be inadequate. Even space scientists are finding their largest computers not good enough for the sheer volume of data relayed from their satellite micro-processors.

Turning the monster off

We are not helpless in the face of all this overload of sound and information. We can do something about it so that our inner self gets some peace. It does take a bit of an effort, but it is not all that hard to do. You may have some withdrawal symptoms when you start turning off the noise in your life. Just as when we try and cut down how much food we eat, and quickly realise that our belief that we can easily control ourselves is a myth. It is always difficult, and takes patience, to form any new habit.

To begin to learn about silence and the inner stillness that frees your spirit, go without radio, television and music for a week. There are other songs and voices to hear, but they are inside you. Here is a daily routine to fortify you for the onslaught of sound and information that will face you as you begin each new day.

Stillness: the morning workout

Learning to be still is to access your inner space. Unplug the phone. Make the room dark. Sit comfortably. Close your eyes. Keep perfectly still. If you want to itch or squirm, resist these impulses until they go away. Let your arms grow heavy, then your legs. Breathe gently. Imagine your whole being as quiet and resting. Let all thoughts float away. Enjoy your stillness. Try it for five minutes, then ten minutes. Do this *every* morning.

Peace and quiet:
healing for the whole self

Think for a moment about those words: *peace* and *quiet*. What magic words, what rare treasures for the average person. What yearnings these words inspire in our busy lives. No wonder they are used over and over again by travel agents who want to sell to the world-weary. We often feel that simply stopping what we are doing to find some peace is an impossible luxury. If you have children you would probably think it a crazy suggestion that you could find any peace, except when they are at school or you drop exhausted into bed when they *finally* go to sleep. It is not without good reason that the usual conversation between two mothers with new babies is all about how their kids sleep.

Privacy, peacefulness, and quiet are the true luxuries in life. These are what the very rich and powerful are seeking when they pay millions for an island in the Caribbean , an estate in Mexico with miles of hills, or a penthouse at the top of a skyscraper. Such places provide the potential for escape from the world and other people into a kind of peace. But this peace is an external one: even in the most ideal of quiet places, a person can still be in inner turmoil. Wisdom knows you cannot run away from yourself.

Stress and depression can affect anyone from princesses to bag ladies. The very latest fashion for celebrities whose lives are falling apart because of their stressful lifestyle is to retreat somewhere and be treated with silence and stillness – often using meditation and other techniques from various spiritual traditions to achieve the goal of reunifying the fragmented self.

There is a place of far greater privacy and peacefulness available to you than a private island, penthouse or health clinic and it is *free*. This sanctuary is waiting for you when you enter the world of your inner self, and the path to it is through silence.

The world of your inner self has been with you from the moment you were born. It is the place where you see that you are an individual person, separate from others, with a unique identity. It is where you can recognise your essential self and temporarily give up your need for self-affirmation, self-realisation and self-fulfilment. Emptied of these manifestations of your ego, you can discover that this inner world is the home of the spirit. Here is the sanctuary where you may find the peace and quiet to sort through your priorities and relationships, relax into what you truly feel, and give yourself space and time in which to make new discoveries about yourself. You may even venture to ask what is the meaning of your life, since no question is too big to examine when you are dwelling in this private, hidden sanctuary of self. This is the process that the ancient Greeks called the *theoria physike* – the vision of the nature of things. It is a way of finding a true relation to self-awareness, giving you the ability to step back from the active you in order to find out what you are actually feeling. It is an ability to transcend the usual perimeters of your ego, what psychologists call being in a state of *metamood*. It helps you use your emotional feelings in an intelligent way rather than in a disorganised fashion. Henri J. M. Nouwen, reflecting on the importance of solitude and contemplation, notes that silence, especially in periods of crisis, conflict and strong emotional tension, can not only offer healing but also show new ways for a life with others.

Silence is a key

Silent silver lights and darks undreamed of,
Where I hush and bless myself with silence.

Robert Browning (1812–89)

Silence is an ancient key to open the inner self. The resulting inner stillness which it can bring is a powerful tool in the process of self-perception and healing. The nature of this silence is important. Hostile silence, of course, can be an emotional weapon, signifying anger, displeasure or disapproval. This kind of silence does nothing for your spirituality. It is a form of punishment that cuts off all communication and can bring feelings of guilt and frustration. You will have shut the door to your inner world, and thus to your true feelings. But the kind of silence which is spiritual in its nature enables us to reach deeply within for hidden resources with which to deal with life. It creates within us a sacred space where we can be alone with ourselves. This is a realm of total privacy, where truth dwells at the heart of our being.

Recently, a successful New York businesswoman told me about a monk she had met on a flight to London. This man made a terrific impact on her. She was intrigued by him and questioned him deeply about his life. Fascinated by his descriptions of monastic life because it was so totally different from her own life-style, she wanted to know 'the secret for getting a spiritual life'. How had he arrived at his spiritual state? Could an ordinary person like herself obtain it – particularly as she was not a churchgoer and confessed to doubts about the reality of God. What was the monk's secret? As a busy woman with two sons and a lawyer husband, she was looking for a quick answer. She wanted a formula or some planned programme that would take her straight to a spiritual life, and give balance and meaning to her existence. She wanted answers to what her life meant *right now!* The monk told her that there was no easy way to get together a spiritual life. He did not have a secret, single way like a diet or a work-out routine that opened a life rich in the spirit. What he had in common with all monks, he explained, was the giving of his life to a search for the sacred – that is to seeking God, the ultimate and eternal truth.

It is this seeking that transforms and informs a monk's life – the true conversion of one's whole life; what is termed *metanoia*. There is no arrival point in this life where monks declare: 'Ah, I've got there! Hello, God!' It is rather that the journey is the important thing. What greatly helps them on this journey, the key contemplative monks use, is silence. It allows them to in-dwell – that is to live out a life that is more of an interior one than one external in the world. So if a monk did have a secret it would be about the power of silence as the way to open the Gateway of Stillness.

Quiet Time – making silence part of your ordinary life

Making silence part of your ordinary life could not be simpler. Each day make a few minutes of quiet time. These are private moments to rest and relax. Ignore all the protests which you may encounter from your busy mind, especially the one which goes: 'I just don't have the time!' Be firm and resolute, but do not make a contest of this routine. Your mind has probably been occupied from morning to night. Being silent and still is a great challenge to it, but once you get the hang of it nothing could be easier.

Make sure everything is comfortable, and darken the room if possible. Turn off the TV and radio, unplug the phone, turn off the answering machine, fax, mobile, and pager. Shut the windows if the noise outside is too much. Don't worry if you cannot make your environment perfectly quiet as this is almost impossible in today's world. Just try to forget these intrusions as best you can by not mentally tuning into them. Do not wish to be somewhere different, since this will make you annoyed. Being annoyed is not helpful to finding inner peace. Allow all thoughts to pass out of your consciousness. Begin to let silence envelop you. If you fall asleep, do not worry. It will do you nothing but good. Lie down on the floor if possible so you do not associate quiet time with going to bed to sleep. Otherwise use a chair or sofa – it's important to be comfortable.

Be very gentle with yourself during this time. Take it slowly at first and make quiet time the exact same length *every* day. Twenty minutes will do, but half an hour is better. If you work at home, try for an hour. This may seem a long time, but it means there is time for your body to relax and for you to settle into the interior stillness that develops. This is not a time for worries, planning, or even fond memories.

Invite the four guardian angels of your senses to help you during your quiet time. The first angel, called Whisper-Not, is the guardian of your mouth, who watches over your lips so that no words come out. The second angel, called Beautiful-Invisible, watches over your eyes to help you keep them shut so that you may see dreams. The third and fourth angels are twins. They are called Gold-Song and Silver-Song and have the hardest job of all because each one guards an ear and tries to make all the outside noises soft and gentle.

Make this quiet time a daily practise which becomes a ritual for you. Rituals which strengthen the spirit are sacred habits. Your body will be grateful for this daily period of inactivity. The historian Thomas Carlyle once wrote: 'Speech is human, silence divine therefore we must learn both arts.' As well as teaching yourself the art of silence, you are also learning not to fear inner solitude, and that you do not need to be constantly occupied by entertainment, distractions, amusements and outside stimulus. There is enough creativity and wonderment waiting inside yourself.

Stillness – the treasure of inner space

The deep stillness that lies beyond the spiritual Gateway of Stillness is not the peacefulness of a great garden where the sounds of the world may be far away. It is not the cloistered silence within monastery walls. It is not the endless solitude of a cell in some forgotten prison. True stillness has nothing to do with our external world, the ordinary world we know. The marketplace with all its bustle and people is actually as good a place for interior stillness as the monastery, for this inner state is the absence of ego. This stillness emerges only when you put to one side all your narcissistic concerns for self. It has the capacity to take any form or shape to accommodate all that is spiritual. It is a purifying state for entering the realm of the sacred.

How do you get this golden stillness, this interior world of silence? First, close your mouth. For once give up the sound of your own voice, which so often is merely talking about yourself. Empty out that basket of conceits you lug around – the ones you think express who and what you are. Be quiet in body and mind. You may use meditation, prayer, or the calming exercises elsewhere in this book to achieve this. Once you are in quiet state, begin to be aware of inner silence.

Such interior silence is not a void. It is an environment full of life. There are sounds and images. These are the voices of our inner life and the dreams and fears we suppress from our consciousness. This inner self speaks of our desires, disappointments, loves and sorrows. It is a place where our hearts may be refreshed by hope. When we turn inward, we enter the place where our true self lives. Here we can be at one with all Creation. It speaks to us in holy voices, songs, chants, poems, dreams, and desires.

The stillness that results from true silence of self can be difficult for an over-busy, preoccupied person. To plunge too quickly into silence may overwhelm your sense of being in control. But do not panic, for there is nothing to be afraid of in setting your spirit free. Your inner world is your self too, the part of you that connects you to the universal and eternal. I usually advise a busy person going on retreat for the first time *not* to go on a silent one where you speak to no one and no one talks to you. Little and often is a good way to begin to use the Gateway of Stillness which leads to the garden where the seeds of wisdom may be planted, and where the harvest is freedom to discover your true self. Some of these discoveries will be pleasant surprises, others not so nice. Each one will bring you deeper into this garden of your soul where your true self waits to greet you.

Using interior silence: important questions, holy answers

When you have attained a stillness of body and mind, for instance during one of your quiet times, and all thoughts of your ordinary life have passed quietly from you, let the inner stillness grow. This is not the end of your journey to the interior. It is only the beginning. Your spirit will arise as if from slumber and unfold your heart, revealing what has been hidden and speaking with an inner voice which belongs to the spiritual aspect of yourself. The spirit has the power to raise up in you a different consciousness, one which can bring new perceptions about your life. This holy dimension of your humanity is a mystical one. It doesn't matter if in this stillness nothing much seems to happen for you – do not worry if there are no inner voices nor a different sense of being. If nothing happens except a flooding sense of peace, you are already in the garden of your soul. This is a true beginning to learning to live a sacred life.

This interior world where stillness reigns is the place to ask yourself the big questions. Who am I? What is the meaning of my life? What do I love? Is my heart kind? What are my true gifts? What are my true faults? Any one of these questions is a good one to begin with. You can probably easily think of a dozen more.

Whatever questions you choose to ask yourself, take just one each day for a week. Keep asking this same question inside your inner space. Ask *in the spirit*: your concern with the truth about yourself and the way you are living your life.

Listen to any other voices that come into your awareness. These are the voices of your spiritual self. Return again and again to these same basic questions because they can help to clarify your life and to lessen your sense of fragmentation. They will help you to live in the present moment and not hunger for what the future holds or for some treasured past. To ask such questions in this way is to make them into a form of prayer, and this leads deep into the garden of your soul. You have been given this place of inner sanctuary to which you may escape as surely as Isaiah was promised by God his escape from Babylon: 'Do not remember the former things or consider the things of old. I am now about to do a new thing; now it springs forth, do you not perceive it? I will make a way in the wilderness and rivers in the desert.' (Isaiah 43:19). New insights will lead you from the confused values and perceptions of the Babylon of the modern world into greater visions of the wonder and potential of your life. These are spiritual waters that renew and call forth the flowering of yourself. Here is 'a new thing' suddenly brought to life. Here in your stillness is 'a way in the wilderness'.

Withdrawing to the sanctuary of inner space can give us strength to face ordinary living by heightening our perception of our present situation, helping us to focus on the truth about ourselves as individuals. It also increases our acceptance and sometimes our understanding of the mysteries which make up our life.

The light and darkness of being

All the visionaries, from Christian saints to Native American shamans, tell us how they experienced a great light when they travelled deeply within the interior world. The light appears to come from within, yet reaches from the present moment of being into endless future. The Absolute or God, the Divine, the Eternal One, is usually described as a radiant light of unimaginable beauty and intensity, different from any light ever known. This experience of light is always sudden, radiant and luminous. St Augustine wrote that when he entered the secret place of his soul he beheld 'the light that never changes'. He said, 'It was not the common light that all flesh can see, but different. He who knows truth, knows this light and who knows it, knows eternity.' Many other saints from various spiritual traditions tell us of this same light. Those who have near-death experiences also speak of it, and those who meditate often enter a realm of light. We are told that when the Apostles Peter, James and John watched Jesus at prayer, a change came over him. His face was shining like the sun and his clothes became dazzling white. He was transfigured by God. Then the ancient prophets of the Old Testament, Moses and Elijah, appeared in radiant glory to talk to Jesus and suddenly from a great cloud came a voice which said, 'This is my Son, whom I have chosen – listen to him!' (Matthew 17:3–5).

This experience of divine light which is of the spirit is not something only for saints and prophets. We are all the elect of God because we are part of a universal harmony, born from and into a divine light. When we are in union with the holy, we are transfigured by this light, which is the light of perfect love. No one can say that the sounds or visions you behold in your inner space are

---

Lighten Up Inner Space

Ask yourself these three questions, which cast light upon the darkness of your being:

1. Where do I find God?
2. What is it I want to say to God?
3. What does it mean to love life?

not divine. No one may claim to know better than another such mystical experience. No one may give such things names or declare with certainty from whence they come. Such things belong to the spirit and the spirit of everything in the entire universe belongs to God, the Absolute.

Practising the presence of God: keeping inner stillness in everyday living

How can we hold on to this inner stillness, which brings us so much peace, when we return to ordinary living? This is a question that troubles everyone who undertakes to live in the sacred. How often such a person thinks, 'If only I could keep this inner feeling with me, if only I could stay as still inside me as I do when I pray or meditate – when I am at peace!'

Some three hundred years ago there was an ordinary young man of eighteen who one day looked at a barren tree and in that moment realised that through the grace of Creation it would soon have leaves, then blossom and finally fruit. This gave him a profound sense of life's providence and power and left him with a great love of God. This young man, who had been a servant, became a monk. In the monastery, he was given the most humble of tasks to do, from cooking and washing up to digging in the garden. He never complained. In fact one day he heard a rumour that he was to be sent away from the monastery which was his only home. He did not despair but said to his Abbott, 'I am in the hands of God. He will do with me as he pleases. If I do not serve God here, I will serve him elsewhere.' He was not sent away – the rumour had been false – but this acceptance by him on where he stood in relationship to the divine was unquestioned.

Now Brother Lawrence, for that was what he was called, had at first found little comfort in prayer. He poured himself and his worries out to God, but remained troubled. In the end he cried out to God: 'It no longer matters to me what I do or what I suffer, pro-

vided that I remain lovingly united to you.' In that moment his
soul opened and all his inner turmoil and pain vanished because
he clearly saw that the answer to all his difficulties was to live continuously in the presence of God. He considered this not at all a
hard task and explained, 'In the way of God thoughts count for little, love does everything.' When pressed to explain what this
really meant, Brother Lawrence replied that it was not necessary
to have great things to do in order to stay in the presence of the
holy. 'People seek for methods of learning to love God. They hope
to arrive at it by I know not how many different practises; they
take much trouble to remain in the presence of God in a quantity
of ways. Is it not much shorter and more direct to do everything
for the love of God, to make use of all the labours of one's state in
life to show him that love, and to maintain his presence within us
by this communion of our hearts with his?' By way of illustration
he declared, 'I turn my little omelette in the pan for the love of
God.' (*The Practice of the Presence of God*).

Can it be that simple? Was Brother Lawrence right? Can you
be with God when you are cooking an egg or washing up? Can
your companion be God when you are stuck in traffic on the way
to work? The answer is very much *yes*! Because all life is sacred,
washing up, doing housework, taking the kids to school and working at the office or wherever are all part of it. Has no one ever told
you that God is glorified in the small works of the hands? Millions
of people everywhere instinctively know that they do not have to
be in a church or other religious building to remain in God's presence. You can make your heart a chapel and go to it anytime to talk
to God. But how do we commune with God on a continuous basis
like Brother Lawrence without the helpful religious structures of
his monastic way of life? We are centuries down the road from his
day. Our cultures are different. We take practically nothing for
granted. We are cyberspace people collectively exercising a degree
of individualism unknown in his day. Is it possible to maintain
myself in the presence of God in spite of all this?

It can be done. Firstly I need to try very hard to renounce whatever does not lead to the sacred, whatever in my life prevents me from living out the fulfilment of my true self, whatever dims the interior voices of my inner space, whatever prevents me from journeying to interior worlds, whatever denies the holiness of me. Secondly I need, like him, to believe in my heart that God is always with me, that the sacred spirit of the cosmos is within every cell of my being and in all that surrounds me, whether it be a living creature or the plants and pebbles at my feet. When I look up, God looks up; when I look down and see a flower, the Divine is made visible. The clouds that pass above me are as alive in Creation as me. Nothing is truly dead, for there is neither beginning or ending. So if God is with me in a way more intimate than my own body, and in all things everywhere, it is simple to be with him as I journey through my ordinary day. But I must keep his presence always in my thoughts, coming back to him from time to time, never completely letting go of this sense of his presence. God must become the beloved dweller in our hearts and the shepherd of all our nature. Daily meditation and prayer help this awareness. Having a set time for a sacred ritual, whether at home or elsewhere, helps. Just sitting down, becoming silent, and entering the Gateway of Stillnesss helps. God is not just in your soul, he is everywhere – so just reach out.

Brother Lawrence insisted that it was necessary to talk to God throughout the day. This was an inner conversation spoken by the spirit. To think you must abandon God to deal with the world is untrue and impossible. You may think God has gone away, but he hasn't. The more you are with God, the more you will be strengthened to do what you have to do. Whenever we consider doing something, we should say, as Brother Lawrence did, 'God, I will never be able to do this if you don't help me!' He warned that a sharp distinction should be made between acts of the intellect and those of the will. The former are of little importance while the decision of our free will means everything. When we surrender ourselves by our free will into God's hands and make him our constant companion, we may not be rewarded with the realisation of all our dreams and desires, but we are protected from self-deception and all those ego trips whose nature is dissatisfaction. It is when you renounce everything which does not lead you to God, the Absolute, that it becomes possible for you to recognise in a fully conscious way that God is intimately present within you.

Thomas Merton (1915–1968), the Trappist Monk and spiritual writer, wrote of this act of faith:

> Until a man yields himself to God in the consent of
> total belief, he must inevitably remain a stranger to
> himself, an exile from himself, because he is
> excluded from the most meaningful depths of his
> own being: those which remain obscure and
> unknown because they are too simple and too deep
> to be attained by reason.

Seven principles for living in the presence of God

1. Renounce all that you believe is not from God.
2. Acts of the will are important, those of the intellect are not.
3. In the life of the spirit, not to go forward is to fall back.
4. Respect life, for death is always near: be prepared for time may be short.
5. Do nothing in meditation and prayer for reward.
6. Bring the sense of the sacred from your inner space into ordinary living by conversing with God as you go about your daily life and everyday chores.
7. Let this practise become a holy habit. It will nourish your whole life and give balance and perspective to all you do.

Brother Lawrence was also quick to point out that such a practice does not mean you have to suffer in some religious manner. 'God must be served with holy freedom,' he wrote. 'We should labour faithfully without distress or anxiety, calmly recalling our spirit to God whenever it is distracted.' This means that we must place our confidence in God, believing that the holy spirit of life itself will not abandon us.

The practice of the presence of God means living with a sense of the sacred all the time. This will enable you to declare with serenity these words of Psalm 131: 'My heart is not proud, nor haughty my eyes. I have not gone after things too great nor marvels beyond me. Truly I have set my soul in silence and peace.'

THE SECOND GATEWAY

Mindfulness – The way of being present to the moment

Mindfulness is a gateway into the garden of the soul because it is the way to tell the difference between human illusion and holy reality. You have achieved perfect mindfulness if you live in a way which values the present moment above everything else. So to live mindfully is to be aware of the reality of yourself in this moment in time. Are you agitated, bored, frightened, happy, having bad thoughts, angry, doubtful, uncertain, upset, or what? Being mindful means you recognise what is going on *now*. This frees your spirit and leads you to your true self. In this overloaded sensory and information age, when we can so often feel lost and confused, using the Gateway of Mindfulness frees you of illusion, helps you shed all the passing cravings and desires which bring suffering and focuses you on the truth of how you are living.

If all this sounds complicated, it need not be. Of course, there are many people who have a moment of holy revelation that connects them instantly with a grand vision of life. But sometimes bringing our attention to the way things are in ordinary life can result in an awakening that is much simpler, though just as direct. This is the practice of mindfulness. For example, just being aware of the pressure of your foot on the ground as you walk, or the feeling of your body as you sit on a chair can lead you inwards to how you are. Perhaps your mind is filled with anxious thoughts. Rather than suppressing them with yet more amusements or activities, you increase your awareness of them, bringing them into the light of spiritual values and finding out what such feelings say about your life. Are they illusions that have no reality? Is there fear to be faced and dealt with so body, mind and spirit are in balance? Such confrontation does not work unless it provokes wise reflection, and a mindfulness of things as they *really* are.

For the Buddhist, such mindfulness underlies the Noble Eightfold Path, which consists of the eight perfections of Vision, Livelihood, Speech, Action, Effort, Understanding, Awareness and *Samadhi*, the state of established being. Perfect Vision, for example, may let you catch a glimpse of an entirely different way of living. Perhaps you can suddenly see the interconnectedness of all life – that the tree in your garden, the stranger in the street, the water in the stream and you are all related in a mysterious but real way. Perhaps you become aware that the task of humanity may not be to discover how everything works but to learn to love unselfishly. Such visions of perfection can affect how you live your life because they communicate how things really are. All the great transformation of your being begins when you live out this new vision. To do this we need to discover a way of living and an understanding of reality that is far vaster than the one we are able to define with the senses of our bodies and the perceptions of our minds. We must become truly awake. This awakening has been described as many things – God, Godhead, Ultimate Truth, the Eternal, Enlightenment, Higher Knowledge, Original Nature. Whatever we chose to call it, awakening to this sphere of consciousness brings a dimension in which we can find a release from suffering into a profound freedom which transcends ordinary living. It will transform your life to find this way of being, this resource for living out your true nature.

All of us carry inside ourselves a concept of self. This can become a dark definition which inhibits our creativity and makes us a prisoner of guilt when we do not come up to our own expectations. Our sense of failure can be overwhelming. So disappointment and disillusion reign in our lives even as we survey the comforts and pleasures surrounding us. In defining myself by the values of the external world and not by the reality of my true self which lies buried in the holy ground of my inner being, I have separated myself from God. I have ceased to be the human-in-the-image-of-God, because my definition of myself does not include *all* of me, or even the greater part of me. I have put myself into a life of illusion and suffering because what I desire is of the human world, which is perishable. I thirst and crave for what is passing and what is passing brings no lasting satisfaction. Do we not know in our hearts that desire is blind and deals out wounds as often as pleasure? True mindfulness holds a key position in releasing us from such a disappointing life. The Buddha declares right mindfulness to be the noble path which leads away from such suffering. Jesus tells us not just to pray but to 'watch that we do not enter into temptation' (Matthew 26:41; Mark 14:38). What is the nature of this temptation? It is when we fall victim to making self-gratification our goal instead of self-realisation. When you believe that only what brings pleasure makes you feel whole and real. When you believe first in your own importance. When you dress daily in the pride of your worldly possessions and accomplishments, believing these define who and what you are. When your self-interest becomes more important than any consideration of the society to which you belong so that you lose all sense of community and union with others. To live this way is to live in a world which is utterly perishable. You will have fallen into a life of personal gratification where peace is impossible, since it is not in the nature of our senses to be satisfied. This is the true nature of temptation. The sacred Hindu scripture, the Bhagavadgita (2:71), puts it this way: 'A person who has given up all desires for sense gratification, who lives free from desires, who has given up all sense of proprietorship and is devoid of false ego, he alone can attain real peace.'

When you live in this state of continual temptation, your body is pulled this way and that. Your mind works overtime to make it all agreeable, but your spirit pulls you in a different direction, saying: 'All this is perishable! You belong to something more. Look at the tree, the stone, the stream, the bird in the sky – you are all these and more!' True mindfulness is the instrument of your release. It is a right receiving in the mind of what is happening and a right responding to that by both the mind and body. You are able to do this when you are in a state of keen attention, the kind of attention which transforms your life from being fragmented into a union of spirit, mind and body.

It is of the greatest importance to understand the meaning of such attention in the context of a spiritual life if we are to separate illusion from reality in our lives. A good place to start this process is in recognising that almost everything in our lives is perishable.

Desiring what is perishable

When my daughter was preparing to go to art college, she decided to submit a painting of strawberries as an example of her work. So I bought a basket of fresh strawberries in the weekly market in our little French town. That was on Saturday. By Monday morning the strawberries had rotted with the summer heat and her painting was not finished. So I went further afield to another market to buy more strawberries. These too had perished within a day, and still the painting was not done. So I went further and further from home each day in search of a basket of strawberries. At the end of the week, nine empty strawberry baskets lay on the floor and her painting was finished. Yet it would never capture the reality of the taste of a fresh strawberry. Her painting was a beautiful illusion. So it is with all things of desiring in this world. Like finding fresh strawberries, we have to search further and further away from our true selves to discover yet another basket of things or friends or lovers who will satisfy our appetites. In the end our lives are like a painting of strawberries – an illusion of the real thing, which perished because that was its true nature. What we beheld could never taste of the true thing. So it is with the nature of our desires. All are perishable except for our spiritual hunger for union with God, because the eternal has no beginning nor ending. It is the invisible reality that does not perish.

It is hard to remember that everything in our lives is perishable. Think of our speech. What we say and what is said to us dominates our consciousness. Yet our words are finite and speak of the particular, and of concepts which are limited by the powers of our intellect and the limited range of our senses. The Buddha seems to have concluded that language was always misleading. Speech sits enthroned in our minds, confusing and limiting the discriminative thinking we need in order to reach out to the supreme oneness of life. It is a prime source of what fragments our lives and leads us this way and that. Speech seduces us into reacting in ways that make us feel unhappy. It is a gift of destruction in the mouths of our enemies and the ill-willed. It can be false wisdom coming from the mouth of a fool. Just as everything that falls on the earth touches and changes it, so human words fall on our minds and alter how we view and lead our lives. In a mere minute enough words can fall to destroy everything you thought certain in your life. The betrayal of a marriage or a nation. The ending of wealth. The dying of love.

But then do we not know deep down inside ourselves that all things change and that our lives are filled with the perishable – no matter how much we want it to be otherwise. The face of someone who dies is forgotten. Worldly goods are dispersed and lost.

The honour men and women accord each other fades, and no one remembers.

Focus

Think of the five most important things in your life. Write them down. Will any of them last? Why? How?

The enemy called 'COMFORT'

How we love our comforts! If comfort was only about soft arm-chairs or lack of money worries, all might be well. Unfortunately we seek comfort in many other ways: we want to be continually reassured of our own worth, for example; and we don't want change in our lives. The latter is also a sign of our essential lazi-ness which the psychologist Carl Jung claimed was the strongest human passion.

Jiddu Krishnamurti (1895–1986), an inspiring mentor who strove to discover how to break the boundaries of personal self-limitation, had this to say about our continual seeking for comfort:

> The urge to be comforted breeds illusion; it is this
> urge which creates churches, temples and mosques.
> We get lost in them, or in the illusion of an
> omnipotent State, and the real thing goes by. The
> unimportant becomes all-consuming. Truth cannot
> be found by the mind; thought cannot go after it;
> there is no path to it; it cannot be bought through
> worship, prayer, or sacrifice. If we want comfort,
> consolation, we shall have it in one way or another;
> but with it come further pain and misery. The desire
> for comfort, for security, has the power to create

every form of illusion. It is only when the mind is
still that there is a possibility of the coming into
being of the real.

(*Commentaries on Living*, ed. D. Rajagopal, Gollancz, 1999)

The variety and nature of our illusions

The greatest illusion is that we think ourselves to be important.
This is the cause of most of the world's troubles. Being true to yourself is better than feeling important. Illusions vanish when you
know yourself. What *is* important is the inner sense of who you
are, not what and who you may be in the eyes of the external
world. If you judge yourself by the values of the world you will be
unhappy, because such values are constantly changing.

The illusion of longing for the past

Do you long for something in the past? Perhaps you sold a house
you loved or gave up a garden in which you found joy. Perhaps you
long for the time when your children were little and you were
needed by them, or when a dawn run before going to work took
hardly any effort? Is there something that sticks in your mind and
refuses to go away? Do you wish again and again for the same
thing?

The world is full of wishes and everyone has lots of them. But
if you are cultivating mindfulness – discarding what is illusion so
you can live in the reality of the present moment – then persistent
longings for something already past is not only a waste of time but
destructive of your efforts to live a sacred life.

The first step in stopping these useless longings is to admit you
have them. When you have identified that particular longing

which is like a ghost haunting you whenever you relax or slip into a sense of peace or when you face a frustration and *wish* things were different, drag it up from your memory into the light of mindfulness.

How to deal with it sounds easy but is very hard. You have to put this longing to one side and stop carrying it around as an active force in your life. Letting it go means accepting its damaging nature. Only a life alive with the spirit empowers this kind of existence. Living in this reality reintroduces you to the hidden and forgotten realms of your own experience. It is in this sense that our spirituality becomes a force of recognition. It enables us to disclose to ourselves the divine presence in our experiences of living. Through such recognition, you can be led to the eternal. You will become holy because you are yourself. This is the true meaning of living in the present. Thomas Merton put it this way: 'For me to be a saint means to be myself. Therefore the problem of sanctity and salvation is in fact the problem of finding out who I am and of discovering my true self.' (*Thoughts in Solitude*).

Now is the time to bring into the light of reality your useless wishing for the past and to recognise it for what it is. This hunger for a moment or thing in the past is impossible to recreate. Nothing can be the same once time has passed. Longing for the past is a great illusion. Have neither guilt nor anger but let your longing go and, in letting it go, step into the present moment of your life. Here is the forgetting that is done without regret. Here is the lessening of your suffering. Here is freedom for your spirit.

Focus

1. Find the thing, person, or occasion from the past for which you long.

2. Bring this longing into your mind. Let it flood you. Feel it in your body, emotions and senses. What does your body say? How do you feel? What is the taste, the vision, the

sound of this longing in you? Concentrate on its nature, which is the hidden reason you have such a longing.

3.Remind your self now that it *is* in the past.

4.Now let it go. Say good-bye to it. You have given yourself permission.

5.Each time this illusion appears in your consciousness, tell it to go away. Do not be seduced into a yearning for it. Spend no time with it. Soon it will fade from disuse.

The illusion of believing in external forces

Do you believe that if just the right person or job came your way that everything in your life would be OK? Do you dream you would be happy if only you won the lottery? That little word *only* is like a knife that slices through your present life. It makes you put off the hardest parts of your journey through life, particularly the ones that are spiritual, because it gives you lots of excuses not to face up to your real self. If you believe that some force – a person, a job, riches, a great sex life – will bring you more than fleeting moments of happiness, you are entertaining a great illusion. Behind that illusion is a deeper and more worrying aspect of yourself – the fear of knowing and accepting yourself as you are at this age, in this relationship, at this particular stage of life. Perhaps you are not destined to be the greatest career woman. Perhaps you will always have some boss telling you what to do. Perhaps you will never be rich or famous – most people in the world are not and yet many are happy. Isn't it high time you accepted your lot in life and just got on with it?

Oh, if it were only that simple, for then we could all be instant angels of perfect righteousness. Unfortunately, our belief in the power of external forces and circumstances ranges from other people to magical symbols and astrological forecasts. We think that somehow one or more of these will change us for the better and bring happiness. This is a persistent illusion that masks our refusal to accept ourselves. Does it matter if you are not some great talent that the world may adore for five minutes? You can sing in your heart even if you are not a rock star. You can love as fiercely and as beautifully as the most legendary lover in history. You can be as beautiful as any mythical creature of your dreams. You can sit in a chair or be disabled and still dance in your imagination across the whole stage of the world and never fall, trip or get a step wrong. Accepting yourself as what and who you are is the first step in throwing illusions out of your life. It is an essential step if you are to find your own kind of creativity, spirituality and faith.

Like it or not, your life is sacred. If you believe this then you must live by the truth that dwells inside you and depend only on the internal forces of your true self found there. These forces vanquish illusion and bring you holiness. Live this way without shame but with great gladness because what you depend upon dwells within and is God.

The illusion of permanence

Dissatisfaction with life nourishes the growth of discouragement and despair, which are both illusions that prevent us from living fully in the present moment. In our search for reliability, permanence, security and predictability we fail to recognise that all these things are transitory. They have a life that lasts only minutes, sometimes hours, hardly ever days. Look around you at the living world. Does a flower have permanence? Does a bird enjoy certainty in its life? What of security? The best secured house can still be robbed by a determined thief. The most guarded heart can still fall hopelessly in love. The only security is that which comes from accepting yourself with as few illusions as possible. Even then, we need to recognise that we are all fragile and that we can neither create this world nor control it. From the universe within you, awash with mysterious chemistry, to the vast galaxies surrounding this small planet, all is in constant change. Since this universal flux is the very definition of existence, permanence does not exist and security is unobtainable. Seeking such permanence and security shows a desire for consistency, and since everything is always changing, the only thing that is reliable is change itself. What is predictable anyway? Think about it. Every weekday morning you have coffee on the way to work at a little café that pleases you, then it closes. One day your mother dies. Another day a stranger enters your life and you find yourself madly in love.

Sometimes when we have a sense of loss or feel resentful, our frustrations seem just a natural part of failed actions and unrealised dreams, of life's stubborn refusal to give us what we think we want, need or deserve. But this sense of loss or resentment can cease to be transitory. It can take up residence in our inner space and, as our frustration grows bigger, anger will come to reign in our hearts. Then we know we have been seeking the illusion of certainty and that the fruits of this cannot result in love or contentment.

The destruction we do to the planet may be due in large part to our deep-seated illusion that there is permanence in life. It makes us believe at some collective unconscious level that no matter what we do to the environment, it will still be there more or less as it is now. We really do know it won't, yet our destruction continues. Gone are most of the great forests. Soon the plants that could cure and heal us will disappear before we have discovered their sacred secrets.

Nothing is permanent in heaven or earth. The desiring of it brings despair and discouragement and leads to a sense of hopelessness. This covers the soul in darkness.

The attaining of contentment

If I wish to know contentment, I must first know when I am discontent. Discontentment is like a hungry lion roaring around inside me, eating away at my happiness, my stillness, and the freedom of my spirit. It denies me a place of inner sanctuary in which I may retreat in confidence and where healing may take place. What brings on this feeling of unease with life? Why should I continue to feel that way even when everything and everyone in my life seems OK? What is this inner feeling of unease?

The basic cause of most discontentment is the constant flooding of the inner self with desires. 'I want this. I want that.' No sooner do we satisfy one craving than another appears to take its place. One desire leads to another so quickly that we can never hope to feel content. When was the last time you could sit back and honestly say, 'My life is OK, things are going just fine. I don't want anything!' We are plagued by the constant marketing of things and situations that lead us to yet more desires. A new car, a better dishwasher, a bigger home. Then there are all the goals we are told we should want, from a more important job to greater wealth. Even worse we are encouraged all the time to question our personal relationships – this has become a staple of public entertainment. Do you have a good enough sexual relationship? Is there enough romance in your life? Are you certain you relate well enough to your children? It is important to ask such questions and others like them from time to time, but should they assail us from outside so often? Surely this leads us to doubt the quality of our life and relationships?

All these desires which we allow into our souls seduce us away from contentment. One way to banish them is to count the blessings you already have in your life. This positive and simple action is a powerful force for interior change. It represents a new attitude to life and helps us ignore those constant calls which plead that more is best and that the new is always better. You can *be* instead of always *becoming*, and open your soul to the contentment that is spiritual and lasting.

Practising mindfulness

How can you practise mindfulness if your senses are always leading you to dislikes and likes and attachments and aversions? The trouble does not lie in the sense organs themselves but rather in the way we allow them to result in desires. We constantly react to what we see, hear or touch with either praise or blame, pleasure or displeasure, compulsion or revulsion. When this happens we can react in many ways – with love, acceptance, delight, grief, sympathy, caution, or in other ways which may be positive. But when these reactions to our senses lead us to be filled with desires, we have made ourselves a prisoner of the fleeting moments of our pleasure. For example, we smell delicious food and desire to eat it, although in reality we are not hungry. Perhaps we see something very beautiful and cannot free ourselves from the desire to possess it, even though in reality it belongs to someone else. Our mind becomes filled up in this way with desires which arise from how we react to our senses.

The source of all this confusion of our senses is our self-consciousness – which is about how we relate to external elements and forces rather than how attentive we are to the inner self, the source of the truth of what and who we really are. It is obviously no good trying to shut out the world or to turn off our senses, even if it were possible to do so. Instead, we need to enable our senses to live in the *here and now*.

The Buddha speaks of 'the peril of the senses', and explains that they are present in every context of our human life whether that context is physical, psychological or social. My senses can stimulate desire and its accompanying elements of frustration, lust, violence, anger, depression, rejection, anxiety, delusion, fear, sexual bondage and the conceits of my egoism that tell me, falsely, that I am important in the ways of the world and not in the ways of God. To be mindful is to be attentive to your senses, neither resisting nor indulging them and avoiding all attachment or aversion to them.

You must see them as tools to help you and not masters of how you live. This vision will take great courage, for there are many ways to perceive anything and how you respond to your senses reveals the self you have created during your lifetime so far. This may not please you. It may even shock you. But awareness will bring a rebirth of your true self and a new beginning.

One place to start this process is to increase your awareness of each major sense. See, hear, touch, taste and smell anew. Avoid any emotional reaction to what happens. True awareness must be observation that is free of praise or censure if it is to lead to mindfulness. Go for an awareness walk to become aware of your senses.

Awareness walking

Use a relaxed pace. Go slowly, with a smile on your lips like a Buddha. Be aware of your breathing. Let worries and desires drop away. Observe colour, sounds, shapes and textures. See with new eyes what was formerly hidden. Awareness is the mark of a tuned spirit, one which is in balance and seeks the reality not the illusion. Make your true intention happiness. Let the path you walk be paved with the gold of inner peace so that each of your steps leaves joy and innocence on the earth.

Internal stimuli affect us perhaps even more than external ones. The inner self brings up memories, fantasies, moods, whims, impulses and plans. It is a bottomless box of chaos. We must learn to be attentive and aware of what is moral and possible in this life and ignore external and internal stimuli which experience has taught us only bring unhappiness and non-fulfilment. Refuse to endure any longer the conflict of ambivalence about what is valuable to you and what unfolds your heart.

The Gateway of Mindfulness is a process of purification by means of detaching yourself from useless things. You will develop the ability to see clearly what is perishable and of this world, and therefore illusion, and what is infinite and universal and therefore reality. As you begin to make mindfulness part of your daily life, you will begin to see the true nature of things and in this way invite transformation into your life. Men and women who are wise in matters of the spirit tell us that the more you relinquish self-consciousness and lessen self-orientation, the more your heart will open in communion with God.

Practising perfect mindfulness

Here is a simple daily exercise to bring you more frequently through the Gateway of Mindfulness. Read the words aloud. Say them loud and clear so that they exist both outside and within you:

> I will withdraw my senses from worldly objects. I will
> set aside the force of greed and refrain from grasping
> to myself feelings, thoughts, perceptions and
> memories, even if they are inspiring. They will
> come. I will let them go. My joy will be in being.

Letting go of everything

Now is the moment in your life to give wings to your spirit. Do it today for now is the moment to let go of everything – ego, values, knowledge, everything. All is perishable. All is illusion. Do not fear, for life itself will sustain you as the leaf is held to the branch and the grape to the vine. Let everything go absolutely and live totally in this moment of eternity. This is the place of unbecoming. This is the moment of no-thing. In such a moment the Buddha was enlightened. In such a moment Jesus was transfigured. In such a moment the stars were born.

In moments of doubt I recall this wisdom of Jesus Christ (Matthew 6:25–30):

> I am telling you not to worry about your life and

what you are to eat, nor about your body and how
you are to clothe it. For life is more than food, and
the body more than clothing. Think of the ravens.
They do not sow or reap; they have no storehouses
and no barns; yet God feeds them. And how much
more you are worth than the birds! Can any of you,
however much you worry, add a single cubit to your
span of life? If a very small thing is beyond your
powers, why worry about the rest? Think how the
flowers grow; they never have to spin or weave; yet,
I assure you, not even Solomon in all his royal robes
was clothed like one of them. Now if that is how
God clothes a flower which is growing wild today
and is thrown into the furnace tomorrow, how much
more will he look after you, who have so little faith!

THE THIRD
GATEWAY

Listening – The way of hearing with the heart

To enter the Gateway of Listening is to truly hear what others are saying and, in hearing them with your heart, you will give your spirit a chance to speak. This generates compassion and opens a dialogue between you and God.

We are the most psychologically self-engrossed of all generations, and the more we are concerned with ourselves, the less we can hear what other people are *really* saying to us. We are drowning in a deluge of words from each other and from our media. Even the street signs telling us how to drive our cars proliferate: at one intersection in London I recently counted twenty-two different signs of instructions to be followed simultaneously. Between the noise in our lives, the constant flow of words being flung at us, and the assault on our sensibilities by advice from every quarter urging us on to yet more personal goals, it is not suprising that we have come to regard silence as a longed-for sanctuary of peace. But the real heartache in this barrage of words is that we let ourselves be part of it. We feel compelled to chatter away as if the more we say the better we will be understood, and as if every little detail of our lives must be explained. Ask yourself if anyone besides perhaps your mother is really *that* interested in you?

This sea of words debases what we say and what others are saying to us because it hinders us from listening with attention to what is being said. What we get is a superficial understanding of where the other person is coming from. What we give back often shows we hardly understand them even when we profess our sympathy. Of course talking is important – it is a defining benchmark of our humanity – but listening is equally important. In Rome on 2 May 1999 Pope John Paul II took the final steps in the process to declare the sainthood of a friar, Padre Pio, known for the Christ-like wounds on his hands and feet from which he suffered for fifty years. When the Pope addressed more than 200,000 people gathered in St Peter's Square in Rome about Padre Pio, he chose to emphasise the ability of this simple Italian friar to connect with people. The Pope said, 'By his life given wholly to prayer and to listening to his brothers and sisters, this humble Capuchin friar astonished the world.' It was not Padre Pio's legendary fights with the devil or his reputed ability to predict the future, or even his reported miracles, that brought him hundreds of thousands of devotees. It was his capacity to really *listen* to what others were saying to him. Padre Pio listened with all of himself. His complete attention in every way was on the person talking to him. The world found this quality so rare that he became a holy person to whom pilgrimages were made. Indeed, his listening astonished the world.

Learning to listen with the whole self

Few if any of us will be saints, but we can all try to listen as the sainted Padre Pio did. Just as most of us have learned not to hear what someone is saying when we do not want to understand them, so we can learn to really listen. To listen with the whole self we need to forget ourselves and to fix our hearts, as we do our eyes, upon the other person. No matter what he or she is saying, we need to listen attentively, our mind free of self-concerns, our body inclined towards the other person. They need to *feel* that we are with them. Remember as you listen that their words are symbols for meanings and little openings to their interior selves. Their words can be keys that unlock our hearts so that the door of love may open wide to them.

The following exercise in listening looks really easy, but I think you will find it hard to do. As far as your own response is concerned, can you stop giving advice? Can you *not* talk about yourself? Can you ask all those questions that you know will get the other person talking? This exercise should be done for seven consecutive days so that you begin to build the habit of listening which becomes an expression of your love and a way of practising the sacred.

Listening exercise:

1. Each day chose one person to converse with. Listen very carefully to what he or she says. Guard your own mouth.

2. Afterwards, write down the highlights of what that person said to you – what you thought was really important to her or him, *not to you*. What were her concerns, worries, sadnesses or delights?

3. Next to these highlights put down what how you felt about each of them at the time. Were you glad for her? Angry? Sad? How did you feel inside yourself? What was your heart telling you?

4. Reflect on that person. Visualise her in your mind.

5. Now take that person into your spiritual realm by saying silently or aloud your own words of hope for her success or happiness. If she told you good news, then give thanks for the blessing she has received in her life. These words of hope and thanks are little prayers. They open your heart and the soul is glad.

It has been claimed that most of our communication is through our body language, and that our words are secondary. So if we want to truly listen, we have to listen with our whole body. We can also learn to be more conscious of the physical attitude of the person speaking to us. Are they tense, defensive, angry, relaxed, embarrassed, nervous, excited, joyous? The body can reveal how we really feel even if we try to hide behind our words.

With close friends there are three things which we should have in full operation when we listen to them. These are confidentiality, intimacy, and accountability. You should not need to promise to hold secret any confidence shared with you. Your reputation for being able to keep a secret should go ahead of you. To be intimate with your friends is to be loving, open-hearted, non-judgemental, and to build up your friend's confidence by the attention you pay to them when you are with them. Reaching out and holding the other person's hand may be worth more than a thousand words of reassurance. We need to be accountable for our reactions and not just say whatever pops into our head. Many a quick word of reaction has ended a friendship. Ten minutes with a friend in which you truly listen to them and share with them a concern for their life is worth hours of banal and meaningless chit-chat when only superficialities are shared. Even if you do not agree with everything you are being told, you can still treat as important all the things dearest to your friend's heart. What people long to feel is that you are with them not just in body and mind but in *spirit*.

I am guilty, along with many people, in assuming too often that when someone complains about the state of their life they want my advice. I know it is usually the last thing they want to hear but I still give it – and afterwards I often regret I did not just listen and keep my mouth shut. As to giving advice, if we listen attentively in silence to our friends and meditate upon how they really feel, we leave open the space within us for God's wisdom to speak. It may be only a word, but perhaps it will be a helpful and wise word when we do speak. It is a goal worth aiming for.

The guardianship of the tongue: An exercise in listening

The tongue has the power of life and death. Who are you hurting today? Who are you bringing back to life? Hard words never bring peace, but loving ones revive every heart. From this Monday to next Friday, treat your tongue like a dangerous flame that can burn down a forest. When you meet friends, listen with kindness but be sparing with your response. Give your silence a chance to embrace them. This will be a sign of your love. Your friends may think you have more empathy with them than they ever thought possible.

Our inner voices

The voice of trust

Many people hear in their inner self a message about their lives that they feel is somehow true. Some people believe this is God speaking to them. Many put the feeling down to intuition. Either way, the feeling nags away at them. It is not always about important decisions or problems. Most people will say, 'It's just a feeling I have ...' Learning to trust this inner voice can be hard. But we need to trust such feelings because they spring from deep within our true selves and are often spiritual in nature. While the message may be to do with how we act in the outer world – important decisions, changes, or the solving of personal problems – these matters can all be spiritual if they affect the way we move forward in our lives and with what degree of honesty we are trying to follow the destiny of our true self. We often opt for what we think will be acceptable to other people and forget our need to fulfill what we sense is right for ourselves. A decision based on what we imagine other people think usually ends in disappointment. Our decision taking needs to stand alone and outside the opinion of others. In that way we can forge a personal code that exemplifies our true nature as an individual. Doing this will enable us to let others be themselves too. If you are living a sacred life, your conduct becomes a way of love for yourself and for others, instead of another exercise for the demands of the ego. We need to listen to our inner voice as much as possible – to keep it tuned up and on standby – and we need to trust that what it tells us is right for our life.

The voice of confession

All of us have a shadow side, one we don't like and try to hide from everybody, especially ourselves. Our dark side tells us we are not perfect, although we long to be perfect. It forces us to admit we have done things of which we feel ashamed. Dark acts of our own making, all those little and big errors of omission which lacked love. What is *sin* but this falling away from the essence of God, which is love? We have put a distance between ourselves and God and this hurts us spiritually. We don't feel quite *right*. The way to reclaim a state of grace is to admit our self-made errors to ourselves so that we are forced to look at them in the light of the counsel of love. This willing confession cleans the garden of the soul of all the garbage we have thrown into it over the day, the week and the years, because it is into our spirit that we bin our sins. The more we pollute our spirit, the less we live a life of love. This is the meaning of the saying, 'Confession is good for the soul.'

One of the greatest example of confession in the spiritual life is that of Aurelius Augustinus, known as St Augustine. Born in North Africa in AD 354, his life and his autobiography, *Confessions*, continues to hold a special appeal for millions of people because he was a great sinner who became, much against the odds, a great saint. Such a story gives us hope that we too can overcome our failings. The first English translation of the *Confessions* was published in 1620 and the book has never been out of print. This intensely personal autobiography, written in the form of a long prayer, has three parts. In the first, Augustine confesses the error

of his ways. This clears the way for him to recognise God's goodness and truth. These two parts form the essential confession of
the soul. In the final part, saved from a life of darkness, he offers
praise for God and gives thanks. So his *Confessions* leads – as it
naturally should for all of us willing to admit our dark side – from
a confession of error to a reaffirmation of faith in the hope and
love of God and, finally, to an assertion of God's universal glory.
Some see Augustine's *Confessions* as first a search for truth and
then his thoughts on the meaning he found. In other words, he *listened* to who and what he was at that moment in time.

Augustine constantly urges us to have humility, saying, 'God
is already humble – and man is still proud'. So it should be with a
humble heart that we clean up the garden of our soul through our
inner voice of confession and once again free ourselves for real
union of spirit, mind and body in God. If any question arises as to
whether we have found a dark thing lurking in ourselves, something needing the light of our confession, then this counsel of love
(1 Corinthians 13:4–7) is the standard which will always help us
to discern the good from the bad:

> Love is always patient and kind; love is never
> jealous; love is not boastful or conceited, it is never
> rude and never seeks its own advantage, it does not
> take offence or store up grievances. Love does not
> rejoice at wrongdoing, but finds its joy in the truth.
> It is always ready to make allowances, to trust, to
> hope and to endure whatever comes.

The voice of hope

Depression and a sense of under-achievement seem to affect many
people. There is hardly a family that doesn't have at least one
member suffering from depression and anxiety – someone who just
can't cope. Unemployment, failed relationships, disappointment

Souvenirs of goodness: the I am OK list

1. Take a look at the last six months of your life. Forget the bad things that may have happened. Think about your partner, your friends at home and work, your family, others you may have met and talked with. What do you recall was a happy moment? Why was it happy for you? Were you *giving* something?

2. What do you think is the most positive aspect of your personality? Do you smile a lot? Do you listen to others? Are you easy to get on with? When you are shopping, do you often see things you would like to get for family and friends? Do people think you really care? If tomorrow was the legendary Day of Judgement, what evidence of your love would you place before the angels?

3. Make an *I am OK* list. Give examples of your goodness. Do not hesitate, because if we were never good, we would never know when we were bad. Let your inner voice speak.

4. Use the *I am OK* list the next time you feel let down or when disappointment and depression threaten. Listen to what each of your good qualities says about your real character – the one that brings your spirit and the spirits of others into the realm of love. Could anything in our lives be more hopeful than love?

in our children, poor health, family and friends moving away – the list of things that assail us would defeat the strongest person. What we need to listen to in the midst of all these common causes of despair is the voice of hope. Here is the voice that brings us back to a balanced view, a renewal of faith in our future and an ability to cope. It is part of our nature to hope, but we often forget to listen to this inner voice when we are down. Hope speaks the language of encouragement. If we examine ourselves we can find the positive aspects of our life, what we have done that is good, and the moments of joy. They are always there if we look hard enough. This is self-encouragement of the highest order, for it springs from the hope that we will live in such goodness all the time in the future and that our life will be balanced and whole.

Even if you are not feeling particularly down or anxious at the moment, it is always worthwhile to call the power of hope into your consciousness. One way of doing this is to write about your own quality of goodness. God may, indeed, love us in spite of our failings, but just think how we must delight him with our goodness, the sign of a life lived in love. Just as God is delighted so our soul is rejoiced and our hopes refreshed.

Listening with God: the heart aflame

God is always around. He hangs in there with us in our daily life. It is like some eternal marriage: for better or worse God does not desert us. This relationship, like a marriage, is based on mutual attraction and love: you are drawn to God and God is drawn to you. God calls our souls forth. He wants us to sing with holiness. He calls each of us to him by a word. This word may be creative, saving, demanding, or a blessing. All religious impulses originate in this word from God. It is like a flaming arrow that pierces the heart and inflames the whole person with a new knowledge of herself and others, striking her into an action, a contemplation, an important decision, or a turning in her destiny. It is as if this burning word was full of meaning for you alone. Revelation comes unbidden and unexpected. It is as mysterious and irresistible as falling in love. No one knows the moment that God will call. Such a word may lead to religious conversion and faith. Such a word can call kingdoms into being and cause temples to fall. Such a word has changed the world. For Muslims, Muhammad the

Prophet brought holy words from heaven. For Jews, Moses returned to his people with God's words written on stone. For Christians, Jesus Christ is the Word that was with God from the beginning and became flesh and lived among us.

Since God calls to us, our primary spiritual attitiude must be one of listening. Not any kind of listening, but an inner listening that involves love, trust, compassion, and obedience to the word of God when it enters our hearts. This forms the fidelity of our listening. We are prepared then for spiritual transformation – a change from the slavery of the things and values of this world to the freedom to be our true self, united and whole. Since God may call us in many ways, we must always be listening like this, ready to receive his message.

Sacred listening: the lesson of the open heart

St Benedict of Nursia was born in Italy about 480 AD, when monasticism had been well established for nearly two hundred years and almost all the leading figures in the Church lived as monks. Yet in the west there was no accepted rule of life for such monasteries. Conditions and regulations varied from place to place. In some the life of the monks was ordered and conducive to a life devoted to spiritual matters. In others their situation ranged from chaotic to scandalous. After studying in Rome, Benedict decided to live in a cave as a hermit. However he was not alone for long. Soon disciples gathered around him and he eventually found himself the head of small but growing religious community. Quickly outgrowing the cave, the group moved to Monte Cassino where they established a new monastery. It was here that Benedict wrote his famous Rule, based on his experience of running a community of religious men. His Rule does not restrict freedom, but rather offers it – the freedom to live among others in love. This enlightened set of guidelines for a community life has been used successfully for some 1,500 years, and is still in use around the world today. The opening of Benedict's great work (*The Rule of Benedict*, trans. Justin McCann, Sheed Huard, 1970) begins, 'Listen my son to the instructions of your Master, turn the ear of your heart to the advice of a loving father.' Benedict's purpose in writing his Rule is immediately revealed. It is about love. Drawing from the Bible, he tells us, 'Now is the hour for us to rise from sleep. Let us, then, open our eyes to the divine light, and hear with our ears the divine as it cries out to us daily.' Benedict asks us to listen with our inner self, this ear of the heart, and to wake our souls from slumber. He asks us to live with a heart open to God and pleads with these words from the psalms: 'Today if you hear his voice, do not harden your hearts.'

Yet men and women do harden their hearts. They refuse to listen to God for fear that his word may somehow interfere with their personal freedom. They always want to be the possessor of the right to choose. But was our conception and birth our choice? Is the moment of our death ever truly our decision? No matter how we concern ourselves with our sense of personal freedom, no matter how successful we become, we still yearn for meaning in our lives. We still ask, 'Who am I?' 'What is the meaning of my life?' The answers to such questions are given with the voice of the spirit. When we hear them we are with God. Indeed, happy are those who hear the word of God and keep it.

The school of angels

The idea of angels is thrilling to me because such holiness moving between heaven and earth and protecting me makes me part of an invisible universe. The very concept seems beautiful and magical and reminds me of Plato's belief that our souls themselves are winged. If there is a special angel whose name most people might recognise, it is Gabriel, the chief of all guardian angels. It is claimed that when an angel becomes visible to a person, this angel is either Gabriel himself or one sent by him. Most people know the story of Gabriel appearing to Mary with the greeting, 'Rejoice, you who enjoy God's favour! The Lord is with you!' (Luke 1:28) As you might expect, Mary was afraid, but Gabriel gently admonishes her:

> O Mary! Look well, for I am a form difficult to discern. I am a new moon, I am an Image in the heart. When an Image enters your heart and establishes itself, you flee in vain; the Image will remain with you – unless it is a vain fancy without substance, sinking and vanishing like a false dawn. But I am like the true dawn, I am the Light of your Lord ...

Winged beings appear in the spirituality of ancient peoples – they may be winged men or, more often, spirit birds. Perhaps the archetypal pagan angel is the Native American Raven. An eerie trickster who brings light into the world by stealing the moon, Raven changes himself as he wants – from a bird into a pine-needle or from a beautiful boy into a terrifying old man. He has elements of all angelic spirits – Prithivi, the Hindu goddess of nature; the shape-changing Greek god Proteus; Eros who pours into us the desires of sexual love; Metatron, the angel prophet who was once the prophet Enoch; as well as Hermes, that naughty trickster of old. He is Logos, Lucifer, Prometheus and Tlingit the owl-man. Raven sits on top of totem poles and is the greatest of all shamans, the one who penetrates secrets.

Many Muslims believe that Muhammad learned the words and gestures of the Islamic prayer ritual by observing the angels. Chinese immortals became angels and took to ecstatic flight, except for the sage Chuang Tsu who saw himself as a butterfly. Butterflies are so beautiful that they just might be angels in disguise. The concept that every believer in God has a guardian angel was taught by Moses and endorsed by Jesus when he spoke of how precious children were to God – 'I tell you that their angels in heaven are continually in the presence of my Father in heaven.' (Matthew 18:10).

Étienne Binet, a Frenchman born in Dijon in 1569, left us a persuasive little essay, *The School of Angels*, which tells us how we will be talked to by angels if only we will listen. He wants us to see that we will hear a sweetness like honey but a truth as fierce as a bee's sting. He reminds us that angels are bodyguards and gentle tutors, although if they chose they could use their immense powers to force us to cooperate with God. Instead, Binet tells us, these divine spirits conduct their instruction with the breath of Paradise. 'They inspire gently,' he writes, 'and so lovingly insinuate their will into ours that they seem to draw us at their pleasure with chains of gold.' An example he gives (from the Apocrypha) is that of the Angel Raphael and Tobias. The angel brings Tobias to his blind father and gives him a cure for his father's affliction. It is an edifying story about alms-giving, duty, and true family life shown at its best when the divine benevolence hidden in Raphael is revealed. Benet explains that we can learn much from the language that the angel uses when he speaks to Tobias. Instead of pushing Tobias rudely and saying, 'Go you there, for God wills it so and beware of disobeying! Go then, for if you don't, you will be made to and at a considerably smarter pace!' Raphael says: 'Little Brother, does it please you that we do this or that?' The rougher language, Étienne Benet tells us, could not be the tone of heaven nor of angels because to order us about would be to deprive us of our free will. We are to be persuaded gently to act in union with God's will and to discern this for ourselves with only some kindly nudges until we get the point. The school of angels then is a school of love. We may hear an angelic voice if we practise inner listening.

Angel lessons

Ask God to be with you. Read one of the following passages, then answer these questions:

1. What does it say?
2. What does it mean?
3. How does it apply to you?
4. What is the *single word* that sums up how you feel at this moment?

Meditate for ten minutes on this word.

The rich young man

> And now a man came to him and asked, 'Good Master, what deed must I do to possess eternal life?' Jesus said to him, 'Why do you ask about what is good? None is good but God alone. But if you wish to enter into life, keep the commandments.' He said, 'Which ones?' Jesus replied, 'These: *You shall not kill. You shall not commit adultery. You shall not steal. You shall not give false witness. Honour your father and mother. You shall love your neighbour as yourself.*' The young man said to him, 'I have kept all these. What more do I need to do?' Jesus said, 'If you wish to be perfect, go and sell your possessions and give the money to the poor, and you will have treasure in heaven; then come, follow me.' But when the young man heard these words he went away sad, for he was a man of great wealth.
>
> (Matthew 19:16–2)

The forsaking of idols

Thereupon [on Judgement Day] each soul will know what it has done. They shall be sent back to Allah, their true Lord, and the idols they invented will forsake them.

> Say: 'Who provides for you from heaven and earth? Who has endowed you with sight and hearing? Who brings forth the living from the dead, and the dead from the living? Who ordains all things?'

> They will reply: 'Allah.'

> Say: 'Will you not take heed, then? Such is Allah, your true Lord. That which is not true must needs be false. How then can you turn away from Him?'

> Thus the word of your Lord is made good. The evil-doers have no faith.

> Say: 'Can any of your idols conceive Creation, then renew it? Allah conceives Creation, then renews it. How is it that you are so misled?'

> Say: 'Can any of your idols guide you to the truth? Allah can guide you to the truth. Who is more worthy to be followed: He that can guide to the truth or he that cannot and is himself in need of guidance? What has come over you that you cannot judge?'

> Most of them follow nothing but mere conjecture. But conjecture is no substitute for Truth.

The Qur'an, Jonah 10:28–36

Listening with the mystics

Mystics are people who have encountered the world of spirit. They have transcended the ordinary consciousness of self and entered cosmic awareness. These ordinary men and women have become extraordinary in turning wholeheartedly to God. Their direct visionary experiences influence and deepen our understanding of the invisible realm of the spiritual. Mysticism is disturbing to most of us because it means surrendering to a power greater than any human force and advancing towards God on a path that defies human reason. Such a person is no longer in command of their own life, their own mind or their own will. Mystics are to be found in most of the world's religious traditions and in the spiritual beliefs of indigenous people. All mystics seem to arrive at the same final vision of the reality of life which is its universal unity – the absolute oneness of all Creation. What such men and women have to tell us makes for sacred listening.

Rumi on a door that's never locked

The Persians called him Jeleluddin Balkhi. He is known to the rest of the world as Rumi. He was born in September 1207 in Afghanistan, but he and his family fled from invading Mongol armies to settle in Turkey. His life was fairly normal for a religious scholar until he was about thirty-seven years old. Then he began to change into a mystic who turned his visions into poems that make the meeting of the soul with God into a profound, sensual, and personal union, as in this one, 'What Jesus Runs Away From':

> The son of Mary, Jesus, hurries up a slope
>   as though a wild animal were chasing him.
> Someone following him asks, 'Where are you going?
>   No one is after you.' Jesus keeps on,
> saying nothing, across two more fields. 'Are you

the one who says words over a dead person,
so that he wakes up?' I am. 'Did you not make
  the clay birds fly?' Yes. 'Who then
could possibly cause you to run like this?'
  Jesus slows his pace.
 I say the Great Name over the deaf and the blind,
  they are healed. Over a stony mountainside,
and it tears its mantle down to the navel.
  Over non-existence, it comes into existence.
But when I speak lovingly for hours, for days,
  with those who take human warmth
and mock it, when I say the Name to them, nothing
  happens. They remain rock, or turn to sand.
Where no plants can grow. Other diseases are ways
  for mercy to enter, but this non-responding
breeds violence and coldness towards God.
  I am fleeing from that.
As little by little air steals water, so praise
  dries up and evaporates with foolish people
who refuse to change. Like cold stone you sit on
  a cynic steals body heat. He doesn't feel
the sun. Jesus wasn't running from actual people.
  He was teaching in a new way.
       (*The Essential Rumi*, trans. Coleman Barks, Harper San
                              Francisco, 1995)

These words speak to me of how my coldness of heart can push
God out of my life and how I can fail to listen to the real message
behind sacred scriptures. Is it because I think myself above being
a student at the feet of a master? Is my conceit that great, that I
should think I know it all? Why don't we hear with the ear of the
heart as St Benedict asks? Rumi's words, 'As little by little air steals
water ...' reminds of me of that old saying, 'Her faith was like a

summer puddle – here this morning, but then the sun came out!'

Rumi is right, of course, when he tell us that not responding to our spiritual existence breeds violence and coldness towards God. We do not 'feel the sun' and the garden of our soul languishes in a darkness that we ourselves impose upon it. We often say we yearn for happiness, but perhaps what we long for is the light that warms up the soul. It is a light that speaks of eternal truths and values. It lights the way for us to discover and claim our own truest identity, quite beyond what the world may think of us. It brings the kind of happiness that is defined by a sense of peace and calm. No one is too old to learn to stop being a cynic. No one has a heart that is permanently closed.

Although Rumi was a Sufi mystic, he had a strong connection with Jesus and it is said that there is a Christian church in Iran where the following words by Rumi are carved over the door: 'Where Jesus lives, the great-hearted gather. We are a door that's never locked. If you are suffering any kind of pain, stay near this door. Open it.'

Let Rumi's poem inspire you to read a few of the parables of Jesus. You might start with the story of Lazarus, Martha and Mary (John 11:1–44). Get up from the cold stone. Stay near the door. Open it.

Al Ghazali on the vanquished self

In the spiritual traditions, *recollection* is a way of emptying oneself and becoming a vessel containing nothing but that which concerns God. Recollection means remembering or simply thinking of an intonation which may be spoken or chanted within the mind – or you may remain silent in all respects. Sufis repeat the name Allah or some other religious formula; Hindus practise breathing, music, singing and dancing; and Buddhists a form of meditation. In recollection you move from forgetfulness of self through to a place where the self is vanquished. There is no consciousness of worship because you are totally absorbed in the object of worship which is God. Both the inner self and the exterior world are precluded from your consciousness. You are seeking to dwell in God.

The Sufi mystic al Ghazali was born in 1058 and was one of the greatest thinkers in the history of Islam. According to his own writings, which include much about spiritual recollection, it was his habit from a very early age to thirst after a comprehension of things as they really are. His studies ranged over every branch of religious science in search of truth. After years of agonising over all these matters, al Ghazali finally admitted that the gap between his way of life and God's imperative as he understood it could not be bridged by intellectual efforts, no matter how brilliant, original or inspired. He came to believe that true faith was a divine gift and that all a person could do to prepare themselves for this gift of grace was to detach themselves from everything and empty their mind of all save that which concerned God. He decided at last to leave everything in his life – family, home, professional and social position, honour, wealth – and devote himself entirely to God. He became a hermit and continued Sufi practises until his death in 1111. He describes how someone can experience recollection:

> Let him reduce his heart to a state in which the
> existence of anything and its non-existence are the
> same to him. Then let him sit alone in some corner,
> limiting his religious duties to what is absolutely
> necessary, and not occupying himself either with
> reciting the Qur'an or considering its meaning or
> with books of religious traditions or with anything of
> the sort. And let him see to it that nothing save
> God most High enters his mind. Then, as he sits in
> solitude, let him not cease saying continuously with
> his tongue, Allah, Allah, keeping his thought on it.
> At last he will reach a state when the motion of his

tongue will cease, and it will seem as though the word still flowed from it. Let him persevere in this until all trace of motion is removed from his tongue, and he finds his heart persevering in the thought. Let him still persevere until the form of the word, its letters and shape, is removed from his heart, and there remains the idea alone as though clinging to his heart and inseparable from it. So far, all is dependent on his will and choice, but to bring forth the mercy of God does not stand in his will or choice. He has now laid himself bare to the breathings of that mercy, and nothing remains but to await what God will open to him, as God has done after this manner to prophets and saints. If he follows the above course, he may be sure that the light of the Real will shine out in his heart. At first unstable, like a flash of lightning, it turns and returns; though sometimes it hangs back. And if it returns, sometimes it abides and sometimes it is momentary. And if it abides, sometimes its abiding is long and sometimes short.

(*Invocations and Supplications*, Book IX, The Islamic Texts Society, 1990)

In recollection, you are seeking a peace that puts everything into perspective. When you dwell in God, your spirit is free from the ordinary concerns of life, so many of which can frustrate, irritate or anger you. They feel less dominant and less important in the measure of your whole life.

Read the above passage by al Ghazali again; then think of what it means to place yourself with God, bearing in mind the words of Muhammad: 'Worship God as though you saw Him, for if you see Him not, yet He sees you.'

St Teresa of Avila on the palace of the soul

When we have guests arriving we clean the house, tidy away all our junk and make things as nice as possible. We want to welcome them with love and care. Since God is willing to take up residency in your life in the temple of your body and the garden of your soul, you must also ready yourself to welcome him there. St Teresa of Avila (1515–82), a Spanish nun whose intense mystical visions are among the most direct, personal, vigorous and down-to-earth ever recorded, reminds us that wherever God is, there is heaven.

> Imagine that you have within you a palace of priceless worth, built entirely of gold and precious stones – a palace, in short, fit for so great a Lord. Imagine that it is partly your doing that this palace should be what it is – and this is really true, for there is no building so beautiful as a soul that is pure and full of virtues, and the greater these virtues are, the more brilliantly do the stones shine. Imagine that within the palace dwells this great King, who has promised to become your father, and who is seated upon a throne of supreme price – namely your heart.
>
> If we took care always to remember what a guest we have within us, I think it would be impossible for us to abandon ourselves to vanities and things of the world, for we should see how worthless they are by comparison with those which we have within us. What does an animal do beyond satisfying his hunger by seizing whatever attracts him when he sees it? There should surely be a great difference between the brute beasts and ourselves as we have such a Father.
>
> Perhaps you will laugh at me and say that this is

obvious enough; and you will be right, though it was some time before I came to see it. I knew perfectly well that I had a soul, but I did not understand what that soul merited, or who dwelt within it, until I closed my eyes to the vanities of this world in order to see it. I think, if I had understood then, as I do now, how this great king *really* dwells within this little palace of my soul, I should not have left him alone so often, but should have stayed with him and never have allowed his dwelling place to get so dirty. How wonderful it is that he whose greatness could fill a thousand worlds and very many more, should confine himself within so small a space.

(*The Way of Perfection*, Vol. II)

Who could resist having their whole being a heavenly place? And what is heaven but the perfect union of you with God in love? This is the state when you are whole and living out a life in which your true self leads the way and when you know that you live by virtue of love. When you desecrate your body, you are not practising love, for you destroy what was made perfect. You do not have to ruin your body with drugs, alcohol, sex or food; you can slowly destroy it through neglecting to live in peace with yourself and with others. This terrible process is recognised by many names: stress, anxiety, depression, anger. We know these are killers. God arrives and finds no peace in your body or mind. Nothing is restful there so he goes into your soul, but the garden of your inner self lies neglected. The flowers of your personal gifts have not bloomed. The waters of your compassion have washed away no one's pain. The paths that lead to truth remain unexplored.

Cut through the jungle of your personal caprices and the distracting preoccupations of life and make ready your whole self for occupation by love. This unites you in God. This is what the mystics taught. Start this very moment the practise of listening to others with your heart and forgetting your self-concerns. This leads you to understanding, and from there it is a short step to compassion.

The only difference between most of us and mystics like Rumi, al Ghazali and St Teresa of Avila is that in their search for God they listened with their hearts. We are all born to be mystics and, despite all the confusion of our everyday lives, sudden and overwhelming experiences of beauty or love, or a new understanding of events and existence, are a striking feature of human life. Thousands of people every day have significant spiritual experiences that change their lives and give them a new vision of their future. Revelation or that spiritual understanding which brings consciousness of God's presence is not just the province of saints and mystics. It is your birthright too.

THE FOURTH
GATEWAY

Meditation – The way of opening the spiritual realm

The Gateway of Meditation is one of the most ancient gateways to the spiritual realm because it leads to heightened concentration and those changes in the mind and body which can release hidden realms of consciousness. It will help you to still yourself so you can increase your interior awareness and escape from the constant external stimuli and transient desires and obsessions which compete for your attention and give you little time to be in the garden of your soul.

While the use of meditation as a spiritual practise has never ceased in the East, the art and technique was mostly lost in the West, certainly to the average person. Yet Christian tradition has always understood meditation as one of the exercises of the spiritual life of prayer. Starting in the 1960s, in the world of the atomic bomb and the cold war, there was a new interest in anything which might provide a new vision of the future, an insight into the meaning of life which was more hopeful and less frightening than the prospect of world destruction. The answers were, as always, to be found in spirituality, and the West rediscovered meditation. Today in Christian spirituality there has been a return to the simplicity of biblical meditation, based on the reading of scriptures or the writing of the early Church fathers; and also growing interest in the use of non-Christian methods of meditation while focusing on the idea of the meditation being animated by the Holy Spirit and based on the revelation of God in Jesus Christ.

Meditation is a way of letting go of your worries and of releasing yourself from the constant activities, ideas and emotions of the mind and the body. It is a way to clear out the unquiet, to clean up the self and to use your inner space to become calm and refreshed so that you can restart your life.

Many people I have met over the years who could have benefited from daily meditation as a way of getting some calm into their lives have been afraid to try it. They seem to think it is some sort of inner state from which they might not return – like plunging off a cliff. In one sense, meditation *is* like a dive into unknown waters, but there is nothing to fear. The physiology of meditation has been well known through centuries of human practise and investigated by modern science if that reassures you. It is a safe and healthy practise.

What happens physically is this – in deep meditation, there is a sharp increase in the alpha rhythm of the brain (that accompanies relaxed consciousness), with a concurrent decrease in the breathing rate and oxygen consumption. The heart rate decreases as well, and there is a fall in blood pressure. The skin has an increased electrical resistance. High lactate levels in the blood, associated with stress, fall during meditation. Yogi masters can use meditation to control and master by conscious effort even involuntary functions of the body such as pulse rate, digestion, metabolism, kidney activity and body temperature.

All meditation has a single common ground which is the turning of your attention inward, away from external concerns which demand your attention. It involves concentrating your mind,

often on one particular object or idea. The mind is slowly cleared
of all thoughts. You let them gradually fade away until your mental involvement with thought is suspended. You then have a
clearer, calmer experience of yourself. Your attention has become
inward rather than outward on worldly affairs. The effect of meditation can best be summed up as a significant release from tension.
Meditation can be a very powerful gateway to self-realisation

There are many methods of meditation that will allow you to
achieve this inner state. Different kinds of meditation may be useful for different purposes or for different people. In some practises
you concentrate on breathing to focus your attention. Both
Tibetan and Hindu spirituality insist on the importance of breathing – some ancient yogic texts tell us that all life is in our
breathing. Other techniques include visualising colour, shape or
form in your mind and keeping your attention on it; or concentrating on a candle or a stone; or on a mantra or phrase which is
repeated over and over again as in Transcendental Meditation.
There is a Zen sitting meditation where there is no object of concentration at all. You just sit and try to be aware of your changing
thoughts and feelings as they pass through your mind. Zen priests
in Japan doing this kind of meditation may increase and sustain
their alpha rhythms more than ten times longer than the average
person who meditates. There are walking meditations, where you
concentrate on your body and the processes involved as you move.
Some meditations even involve vigorous whirling and dance
movements, as in Sufi religious practice.

The most immediate benefit of any meditation should be that
you feel more calm and relaxed. It is an excellent way of combat-
ing stress. It should increase your ability to concentrate and
generate a feeling of a calm centre from which you may direct more
of your energy into living more creatively in your personal talents
and gifts. As we discover more about ourselves, our tolerance of
others usually increases. Meditation can take you into different
aspects of consciousness where new insights may come to you.

Today meditation has gained so much credibility with people in the West that it is popular with millions of people, and increasing numbers know something of what it is about. Even the medical profession has come to recognise its therapeutic value, although it is still rare to find a general practitioner who recommends meditation to a patient suffering from stress. In spite of this, some people still find the idea of letting their minds go a very scary thing. They may read about doing meditation in a popular magazine, but actually getting down to doing some is another matter.

The rituals that may go with meditation are also regarded with suspicion by some Christians. Many churchgoers see meditation as anti-Christian, forgetting or not knowing the heritage of their own religion. Others fear being 'taken over' if they are involved in any ritual like breathing exercises or focusing on a lighted candle. Our fear of the unknown is deep and abiding. Yet the unknown is always present in life from the hidden motives behind our actions to the events in the future that none of us can foretell. Rituals too are an everyday part of life, and serve social, psychological and unifying purposes. Our lives contain a multitude of them – from the way we set the table, how we always straighten our desk before beginning work, the village fête. They also serve our spiritual purposes. The rituals or practices that go with a meditation are important ways to focus on your feelings and values, so that through meditation you can reach your inner world, where new discoveries about yourself wait for you.

Christian meditation

For Christians meditation is understood as one of the exercises of the spiritual life of prayer. This is distinct from living a life of virtue and making your faith visible through charitable works towards others. According to the Bible and to Jewish religious tradition, meditation as a practise or technique is based on a repetition of words and phrases, a kind of mantra. In this century there has been a return to meditation by Christians in the form of contemplating a passage of the scriptures or the writings of the early Church Fathers. Such readings should lead to prayerful and contemplative thoughts about yourself, your way of life, and the state of your relationship with God.

There are a number of meditation practises that have been developed within the Christian tradition, which focus on the Gospels, but non-Christian methods are also widely used. Even today, some Christians still have difficulty in coming to terms with meditation practices borrowed from other faiths such as Hinduism and Buddhism. If you are a Christian, reassurance is to be found in Anthony de Mello's definition: 'Meditation is a prayerful state, animated by the Holy Spirit and based on knowledge of the revelation of God in Jesus Christ.' (*Praying Body and Soul: Methods and practices of Anthony de Mello*, Gabriel Calache, The Columba Press, 1997).

Many Christians use some form of Transcendental Meditation as a way to achieve deep relaxation. This relaxation is a preparation for prayer but not a substitute for it. Other ways of easing a state of stress will also work. The whole point is not to treat meditation as a point of arrival in the spiritual life but rather as a gateway into the garden of your soul. That is your destination. As you pass through this holy gateway, you discard the external worries and concerns of the world. You leave the temporal and temporary behind and enter the freedom of true self.

Healing with meditation

Sadness

> 'If you want to get rid of something, you must first allow it to flourish.'
>
> Lao-tzu, *The Tao Te Ching*

When someone says their heart is heavy, we know they are sad. Yet we can be that way and not even realise it. It can be a hidden cause of our unhappiness. If you let your mind wander into the past you will soon discover if you are sad, for the memories that surface will be of loss. Sadness comes from disappointments in your life and that includes being disappointed with yourself. This usually stems from having expectations of ourselves and others which are too high, and desires which inflame our ego and don't do anything for our sense of peace. Meditation is a way of going into your sadness and, by being within it, understanding its nature and being done with it, for it is a dead thing. Say good-bye and be healed.

Anxiety

> 'Riches are not from abundance but from a
> contented mind.'
>
> Hadith, *Sayings of the Prophet Mohammed*

We all know anxiety. It is a natural reaction to fear, anger and stress. Our body chemistry has an automatic biological system for dealing with anxieties – chemicals and hormones rush about your body and make certain you are ready to flee from any threat. The demands of modern life mean we are in anxiety overdrive most of the time. 'Show me what a man fears and I will show you what he is', is an old saying, but the solution to the threat of anxiety is not to find courage to face the enemy – that is a practical weapon for other situations. To confront and deal with anxiety you need to enter a state of calm. In quieting the mind, you set the body at ease, its chemistry changes, and the anxious state subsides. For some people just a few minutes sitting quietly will restore them. For most of us the stresses that flood our lives are so constant that we need to take stronger measures to restore a sense of balance and peace. Meditation is one of the most outstanding techniques that can help you to do this. This is widely recognised nowadays. If you already know it, why haven't you started to meditate? Today is a good day to be healed.

Spiritual desolation

Spiritual desolation happens when we turn away from the positive in our lives. Sometimes we become negative in such tiny ways that we are unaware of it until these negatives collect together like drops of rain and flood us with a sense of desolation. We then feel nothing is worthwhile, that life has no meaning, that all we do is futile and all our efforts at happiness are in vain. Our frustration and hopelessness grow so enormous that we decide finally that God, if he existed in the first place, has gone away.

This is spiritual desolation and it relates to the promise of God. In our despair we have forgotten the universal and eternal aspect of our life, neglected the hope that knows no beginning and no end, and thus denied love. Hope and love are the promises of the eternal in our lives. The important thing when you feel such spiritual desolation is to return to God as quickly as possible. Meditation facilitates this flight from the desert of self back to the sanctuary of inner space where you may recover in the embrace of the spirit.

Basic meditation

One of the greatest obstacles to interior peace is nervous tension. Ten minutes spent releasing your tension before beginning each day will assist you in your daily life as well as when you are seeking to enter spiritual realms. The following exercises will help you begin to meditate.

Feeling is not thinking

This is an exercise to get in touch with bodily sensations. First sit comfortably in a chair. Close your eyes. Feel your back against the chair, then your chest as it expands with each breath. Become aware of your arms, then your legs; feel the soles of your feet touching the ground. Visit different parts of your body. Visualise them. Gently relax them. Sit now within the calm embrace of your body.

Simple focusing

Here is an easy way to get yourself relaxed. Sit with your eyes closed for twenty minutes in a room which is quiet, breathe regularly, and keep repeating aloud (or inside your head if this would disturb someone else) a single word like *peace* or *one*. If thoughts interrupt you, ignore them and continually re-focus on the word you have chosen. If you are on a retreat try doing this each morning and at the conclusion of any talks or between items in the retreat programme. Finally, do the exercise just before going to bed at night.

Chi awareness

The Chinese art of T'ai Chi Ch'uan springs from Taoist physical culture and has been handed down for some 10,000 years. It is a proven way of improving health through stimulating the flow of energy through the whole body. This brings tranquillity to the entire nervous system and, through its demand for concentration, a deep sense of peace. It is a system of meditation practice that is meant to lead to the ultimate harmony of the entire person and a balance between feminine and masculine forces – the famous *yin* and *yang* medical and philosophical concept. The word *chi* means intrinsic and ultimate energy and comes from the Chinese word for air, energy, power or life. The simple warming-up and breathing exercises of T'ai Chi Ch'uan will help prepare you for meditation.

Breathing exercise

This exercise can be done standing or sitting. If you sit, you may use either a chair or sit cross-legged on the floor, putting your left leg outside your right one. Then relax your entire body. Let go of all the worries and thoughts drifting in and out of your mind. Now imagine an invisible string pulling up from the top of your head to an invisible point high above you.

Place your hands flat on your abdomen and, while keeping yourself upright, let your shoulders drop as low as they will go. Take a deep inward breath through your nose, not letting the air fill your lungs and chest but allowing it to sink deeper so your belly swells out. You are sending your breath deeply into the area beneath your navel. This lower abdominal breathing, called 'tan t'ien chi hsi', not only activates vitality in your gut, but the expansion and contraction of the abdominal muscles acts as a massage of the area. This improves blood circulation to your liver and helps your body metabolism.

Having sent your breath down to the belly, which in Chinese alchemy is called the 'lower cauldron' – an appropriate name since this area is traditionally considered an energising centre of your being – you now exhale through your nose. As you do so, press your hands firmly against your belly so that you force the stale air out through your nose. Repeat this sequence six times.

Body consciousness

We are simultaneously aware and not aware of our bodies. Some think a state of good health is the total lack of any awareness of the body – if nothing is malfunctioning why should we feel anything? Others disagree, believing that the loss of a sense of our body causes all sorts of emotional problems which can result in physical illnesses. It is true that the body in good health just gets on with its job, but it does send out signals when it is tired or something more dramatic is going wrong. It may resort to pain or even collapse in a bid for our attention. I have discussed the need for body consciousness in the context of the spiritual Gateways of Stillness and Listening, but such awareness cannot be separated from any aspect of our spiritual life. To live a sacred life is for the whole self to be united and not fragmented – our awareness becomes all-encompassing. Learning to be conscious of your body in meditation is a way of releasing consciousness *into* the body so that which is physical achieves sensory calm.

Stage 1 – Releasing body tension

This approach is based on the technique known as *autogenic training*, in which you train your body to respond to mental imagery. (This is not unlike some of the techniques used with cancer patients where they visualise their tumours as part of the healing process.) Having sat quietly and done the chi breathing exercise given above, you now begin releasing deep tensions.

Put each hand, palm down, flat on your knee: right hand on right knee; left hand on left knee. Keep your breathing gentle and regular and your eyes closed.

Now begin to visualise each part of your body. Start with your right leg and as you visualise it, repeat silently: 'My right leg is heavy and warm.' Repeat this phrase five times. Now do the same thing for your left leg; then your right arm; and your left arm. Think now of your abdomen – the centre of yourself – and repeat five times: 'My stomach is warm.' Finally, visualise your head and face. Repeat: 'My head and face are warm and relaxed, warm and relaxed, warm and relaxed.'

Now, beginning again with your right leg, do the whole exercise again.

Stage 2 – Emptying your mind

Making your body quiet is relatively easy compared to trying to empty out your mind, for our minds are like self-filling cupboards – no sooner opened and an item removed than you find two more in its place. These items are thoughts, worries, desires and memories. Useful as they can sometimes be, a mind stuffed with them is a consciousness that cannot see the wood for the trees. A mind emptied of useless things is a mind free to contemplate God. This is a Zen breathing-counting exercise to help you clean up the cupboard:

Sit comfortably. Close your eyes. You touch nothing. Your lips taste nothing. You smell nothing. You hear nothing. Keep perfectly still. If you want to itch or squirm, resist until the impulse dies away. Imagine your whole body as quiet and resting. Count one as you breathe in. Count two as you breathe out. Continue up to ten, then begin again.

Stage 3 – focusing your mind

> We work with being, but non-being is what we use
>
> *The Tao Te Ching*

Concentration clears the mind of the coming and going of too much activity. It can be learned, and when practised regularly it will quickly develop into an advantageous skill. You develop it by focusing your mind on a single subject to the exclusion of all else. To do this, you must anchor this point of attention in the present moment. What you chose to focus on is up to you. It can be a visual object, say a flower, a lighted candle flame, a leaf, a symbiotic shape, a cloth of pure colour. It can be a sound that you listen to or even one you make, such as 'Om'; or a phrase of prayer, or a mantra.

Once you have chosen your anchor, focus on your breath as it comes into and leaves your body.

Or you can count your breath in and out, as in the exercise above. The intention in spiritual concentration is to cultivate a non-distracted and undivided point of attention. It is in our nature to have a mind full of different thoughts, images, colours, plans, sorrows, joys, memories and ambitions. Some linger, some speed through, but all need to be put aside in meditation so that the mind is focused in complete singularity.

Stage 4 –Withdrawal to your interior world

Having prepared for meditation with various exercises, and by understanding something about its nature, you should be able to begin using it to withdraw to your interior world. Such a withdrawal prepares the way for all the activities of the spirit. It makes you ready to contemplate the eternal. You arrive in the garden of the soul in an altered state of consciousness. This is the purpose of meditation.

In the beginning, try meditating for ten minutes, then gradually increase this to fifteen, twenty, and finally to as long as you want. At the end of each meditation, when your mind is clear and your body relaxed, you may want to repeat an affirmation to yourself (see 'The Eighth Gateway') or simply think of something important to you at this moment. Answers to problems can often appear after meditating that, before you started, seemed to have no solution. Meditating is a habit. You need to practise it often so it becomes one.

Simple meditation exercise

1. Find a secluded and quiet place, and choose the same time every day for meditating, preferably early morning when you won't be interrupted.

2. Choose a comfortable sitting posture.

3. Set a minimum time for your meditation, say between 15 and 45 minutes. Keep to this time *every* day.

4. Let the tension go from each part of your body.

5. Begin to breathe deeply and regularly.

6. Now enter your chosen meditation practice. The following two meditations can be used to start with until you find one that you feel particularly suits you spiritually.

Flame of life meditation

This is a good everyday meditation, but it is also especially
appropriate if you are on retreat or taking time for your inner
self. Do it each evening before you go to bed; it will help you
to slip more easily into restful sleep. But don't forget to blow
the candle out before dozing off!

1. Settle yourself comfortably in front of a lit candle.

2. Gaze at the candle and let your mind and body relax. Do
   not look around the room. Fasten your thoughts on the
   candle.

3. Let your body sensations float away.

4. Close your eyes and sustain the vision of the flame.

5. If other thoughts begin to come into your mind, even if
   they are about light in a spiritual way, open your eyes.

6. Repeat the whole process until you can again close your
   eyes and see the flame.

As your ability to concentrate deepens you will discover that
you need very short contact with a candle (or other object) in
order to focus yourself and empty your mind of thoughts and
images.

Sacred naming meditation

Names and naming are important in all spiritualities. The name
of something is commonly thought to incorporate the sense and
spirit of the thing itself. In this way the name becomes a vessel for
the sacred and a way to enter the realm of the spiritual. The repetition of a sacred name has strong powers to invoke a change in
our consciousness and to facilitate our entry into spiritual realms.
It is like knocking on the door of our soul, which opens to welcome us when we repeatedly call, chant or sing. In Christian
meditation the name Jesus Christ is a powerful instrument of spiritual invocation. You do not have to be a Christian to call upon
Christ in this manner, because when you use the name Jesus rev-
erently and in the hope of the eternal, you are calling forth the
unlimited power and grace of the holy. Jesus confirmed this when

he said, 'Truly I tell you, if you ask anything of the Father in my
name, he will give it to you.' (John 16:23). When the Apostle
Peter was asked for alms by a crippled man, he called on the name
of Jesus to give him instead the gift of a healed body: 'I have
neither silver nor gold, but I will give you what I have: in the name
of Jesus Christ of Nazareth, stand up and walk!' (Acts 3:6).

When in great danger or profound despair, we all appeal to
powers beyond the human realm. Regardless of our beliefs, we usually cry out the name of God. It is our last appeal, and always to
something beyond humanity. We call on the spiritual world, to the
great avatars such as Jesus Christ, Buddha and Krishna: manifestations of the help of the infinite God. Mahatma Gandhi
preached that when fear is lost, any illness is cured by means of the
name of God alone. For Jews the name of God, *Yahweh*, stands for
protection, greatness, fame, glory and refuge. For Native
Americans a person's tribal name has deep shamanic meaning,
linking them to their destiny, to the Great Father, and to their
relationship with the cosmos.

Choose a sacred name to concentrate on. This could be Jesus
Christ, Krishna, Buddha or any other which accords with your
idea of the presence of God. If your sense of the eternal has no particular identity – or even if you believe in no personification or
name at all – you can use the name and sound *Om*, which has an
ancient tradition of spiritual power in calling forth the sacred. I
have used the name *Jesus*.

1. Begin by invoking the Holy Spirit of life to be with you.
   Do this by saying from your heart: 'Come, Holy Spirit,
   dwell within me.'

2. Next pronounce the name of Jesus with the different
   attitudes or feelings you find within yourself. What do you
   feel? Is it anger, love, trust, joy, sadness, disappointment or
   adoration? Let such inner feelings be drawn out into the
   name *Jesus*.

3. Let these feelings swell within you, then dismiss them
   from your mind until nothing is reverberating in you that

belongs to your ordinary life. Gone are worries, problems, resentments. Gone is anxiety and stress. You have handed all these and more over to someone else now.

4. Repeat the phrase 'Come, Holy Jesus, Come, Holy Jesus' over and over again in a chant until all you hear from within your self is the sound made by your naming. In these words you have the resonance of Om and in 'H' the sound that the breath makes in its passage through your body even before you form the name of Jesus itself. Let this holy name become breath itself.

5. Focus your naming chant in order to transcend your concerns of this world until you enter the awareness of your inner self.

6. Continue chanting 'Come, Holy Jesus, Come, Holy Jesus' until it becomes the very pulse of your being. You should begin to feel at one with the chanting and gradually have a feeling of floating, almost as if you existed solely within the chant itself.

7. Now, stop chanting. Be very still in your inner world.

8. Listen with your heart. In the silence of inner space, the name you called may answer you; such a response will be holy. If there should be an inner vision, see it. If there should be words which come to you, listen to them. If a sense of calm arrives, hold it. Do not be afraid for these are states of grace and such grace is from God.

9. Continue to hold this meditative state until it gradually passes and you feel returned to an ordinary state of awareness. You should feel refreshed and renewed by your journey to the sacred.

The path of yoga meditation

Yoga classes are available throughout the West. There is hardly a small town that cannot offer a weekly session of yoga. Most of the people going to such classes go for exercise, seeing yoga as a way of keeping fit, which of course it can be. Although most yoga teachers tell them, students often forget all about yoga as a way to awaken the spiritual. They rarely get beyond learning to do the various physical movements and, of course, these are good for you in themselves.

Yoga is an umbrella term that includes many different philosophical expressions and a multitude of different physical techniques, but it stems from the Hindu faith and teaches that the real purpose of life is to know God and that this knowledge becomes possible when the latent spiritual faculties of the mind are awakened by the practise of meditation. The sage Sri Mangalnathji summed it up this way: 'God-realisation is the purpose and goal of life; perfection, everlasting peace and freedom are its fruits. When God-realisation is once acquired, there is no fall from this exalted state of consciousness. There is no gain higher than this.' So the purpose of meditation is to raise the level of your consciousness to the realm of the spiritual where you can see that there is no separateness in life, that all this biodiversity of life is but one. You are the bird. The bird is you. You are the grain of sand. The grain of sand is you. The higher states of spiritual illumination will bring you a vision of the universe as a single continuously expanding and interlocked whole. Nothing of itself can be separate.

In Chapter 11 of the Bhagavadgita, Arjuna asks Krishna (or God) to reveal his true divine nature. Arjuna is overcome with wonder by the awesome cosmic spectacle that unfolds before him. Bowing low before Krishna, he dares to speak:

Ah, my God, I see all gods within your body;
Each in his degree, the multitude of creatures;
See Lord Brahma enthroned upon the lotus;
See all the sages, and the holy serpents.

Universal Form, I see you without limit,
Infinite of arms, eyes, mouths and bellies –
See, and find no end, midst, or beginning.

Crowned with diadems, you wield the mace and
discus,
Shining every way – the eyes shrink from your
splendour
Brilliant like the sun; like fire, blazing, boundless.

You are all we know, supreme, beyond man's
measure,
This world's sure-set plinth and refuge never shaken,
Guardian of eternal law, life's Soul undying.

Progressive exercises in meditation

If you have practised simple meditation for some time and feel
that your practise of withdrawal has led you to sufficient self-sur-
render, then in yogic terms you have attained a degree of
non-attachment to what is passing. Try this sequence of exercises
for entering deeper levels of true meditation. They are designed so
that you move from the deep relaxation of *asana* into the state of
withdrawal of *pratyahara* and from there into the concentration of
dharana. From this last state you may move into *dhyana*, which is
to continuously be in interior space. Here *samadhi* begins, which
happens when you exist in that contemplation which the mystics
shows us leads to true knowledge of self and the divine.

1 Asana – Posture

This is the practise of deep relaxation. If you have been trying the techniques in this section of the book, you will have done this exercise before. So now do it again – this is what practising is about.

Sit comfortably. Be free of distractions. Align your head, neck and spine in a straight line as if, in the t'ai chi manner, a string connects the top of your head up to the sky. Maintain your position without moving. Relax by breathing deeply and slowly while silently repeating in your mind the sound of *Om*. Say half the sound while breathing in, the other half while breathing it out. Your muscles and nerves will relax as you breathe like this. Soon you will be perfectly still in your sitting posture, yet completely relaxed.

2 Pratyahara – Withdrawal

You now let all thoughts go which stand in the way of your spiritual passage into the garden of your soul. You are not, however, some inert being, because while at peace and in stillness, things of spiritual value will arise.

3 Dharana – Concentration

You are now ready for *dharana*, which is a Sanskrit word meaning to maintain or support something. You are now going to support yourself in your spiritual state by concentrating your mind on a single object. Visualise a flower: its size, shape and colour. Reduce these in your imagination to a fine, concentrated point of shape and colour, as if all you can see is the surface of a petal.

4 Dhyana – Continuous meditation

As you continue in this interior focus, the object you are concentrating on, and your consciousness of the external world, disappear. You are now in a state of continuous meditation or *dhyana*.

5 Samadhi – Contemplative communion

When in this meditation you become free from all senses, thoughts and objects, even of the state of meditation itself, you may enter contemplative communion or *samadhi*. This is a state of being in which there is loss of all subject–object consciousness. It is the moment of the disappearing ego.

The purpose of meditation is to move us foward in our search for the vision of the hidden self. It is a technique for purifying and awakening the spirit and is not, in itself, a form of spiritual salvation. You will not find meditation to be a *final* answer to anything. But it is a classic gateway to the garden of your soul where the answers to your quest are waiting for you.

THE FIFTH GATEWAY

Loving – The way of seeking reality

Love solves all problems, opens all closed doors.

Sheikh Muzaffer, Sufi master

The Gateway of Loving is very difficult, for we are all filled with self-importance and self-interest, both hindrances to love. Our desires can make us confused about how we really feel, and our habits of over-consumption or anger may mask our real need for love and understanding. Often we simply do not know what it is we love. To live a life dictated by love is a continuous challenge because it demands we understand the reality of our strengths and weaknesses and accept them, and that we embrace those we find in other people without judging them. This is to recognise human failings and not see them as faults. It is to see loving yourself as right and as a precondition for loving others. To love in this way is to be faithful to your true self and to allow that right to others. Loving is also both connection and separation in our daily lives: It makes the intimacy of close relationships sweet, for example, but also gives us the strength to let go of those that have failed. It can open up your talents without leading you to use them as a means of control over others. It can bring you the wisdom that makes your sexuality a deeply nourishing gift to another because it is the giving of yourself. Love takes so many forms that it evades definition but at its heart is a compassion that yearns for the triumph of all that is good.

'Where there is no love, put love and you will find love', wrote St John of the Cross, the great poet and mystic of Spain, in a letter from Madrid in 1591. He felt that evil arises from our earthly desires: these prevent us from putting love into our lives and into our relationships with others. Our many desires make us uneasy and we become confused about how we really feel. From such confusion our good intentions become soiled. When this happens we are so weakened that darkness is cast over our spirit. We want to love, but somehow it all goes wrong.

It is this basic yearning to love that is the key to the reality of loving, where you live by love, you are defined by love, and your values are those which come from love. Whatever it is in our lives that we wish to know well, we must love. You cannot master music, art or any profession unless you love what you are studying. If you understand this, then it is also clear that the whole path of love in your life must be rooted in knowing and accepting your true self. To love yourself is your first generous act of loving. When this happens you begin to know yourself and to accept your strengths and weaknesses. From here you can build that tolerance and understanding of others which makes you generous to them as you are generous with yourself. Without this primary love of self which leads to a heart felt acceptance of all others, there can be no sacred living. The Sufi master, Jami, said, 'You may try a hundred things, but love alone will release you from yourself.'

What we are released from is the ego, which rules the mind and does not want our consciousness of God to surface nor our hearts to be filled with love for others. Your ego hopes that your earthly desires and illusions of self-importance will continue to rule you. But if you are to live a sacred life and discover how to live at peace, then love you must. The heart without love is a stone. The heart open to love is a mirror of God.

Love of self: affirmation or affliction?

Our struggle for identity is a powerful personal force which is aggressively fostered today by society. It most often results in no more than a superficial display of conformity to the latest fashion in behaviour for family life and personal and work relationships. This does little to help us grasp the weaknesses and strengths that make us uniquely individual. Equally, we live in an era when the pursuit of physical, mental and emotional comfort seems to be a major factor in how we behave. This also does not help the process of self-discovery, because it encourages us to avoid the potential discomfort involved in confronting our weaknesses.

Many people find it hard to understand that in loving yourself you are freed to love others. Learning to love yourself is an inner process of becoming who you really are, in which you accept and affirm your strengths and weaknesses and in doing so, learn how to give the same kind of acceptance and affirmation to other people. This capacity to relate is an essential vehicle for loving and a central dimension of sacred living. Truly loving ourselves is not a self-centred activity that inflates our ego. It is an act of compassion for ourselves that starts deep within and goes from there outwards to other people.

If we are all part of God, then we cannot judge or hate part of God as being unworthy. We need to put aside any feeling that loving ourselves is wrong We must accept that a precondition for self-love is self-knowledge, even though achieving this may make us feel uncomfortable. We should examine our faults and discover our strengths without exaggerating either out of proportion, because what we are seeking is reality and not illusion.

Contemplating human frailty

To be human is to be a fragile being exposed to many frustrations. When these are transitory, they do us little harm. But when we let them take root in us, they destroy any sense of wholeness. For example, greed (a continual sense of desire), ill-will towards others, anger, dullness of being, restlessness or continual worry, jealousy, lust and doubt are all personal failings that can make the spirit a prisoner and bind up the heart. When they possess us, they can destroy us physically, emotionally and spiritually.

I believe the greatest pitfalls for many people are anger, lust and over-consumption. I suggest you meditate on each one for a week as a preparation for entering the Gateway of Loving. Look at your relationship to each of them, how your own life may be afflicted by them, and how they may hinder your spiritual fulfilment.

Anger

Anger and rage are part of human nature. They exist not because of evil intentions and circumstances but because we are human. The British psychoanalyst Donald Winnicott believed that the rage to destroy when we feel envy and hostility can be a sign of maturity as long as we are able to admit such feelings and take responsibility for them. This kind of self-knowledge shows a high degree of personal integration. However, the problem of anger is not a simple one. The reasons for it may be so deeply buried in you that you have not the slightest idea what your anger is about. You are just *angry*. The extreme of rage is a violence of our nature that can bring death, although most of us control our rage so they we can live in a human group. Most of us also manage to control our anger most of the time. Or at least we think we do until it comes out, usually through our mouths. The most powerful expresser of our anger is not our fist but our tongue. Here is the instrument of life and death: by it we praise or condemn, lavish love or hate. Your spirit knows that hard words never bring peace but loving ones revive every heart.

Ask yourself who you hurt today. What words came from your mouth that went like arrows to wound and cause pain? Ask yourself why this anger is inside you. Where is the source of this burning? What fuels this unhappiness in you? It is usually the loss of love, the sense that we have been rejected. Has your heart become unforgiving and mute because the love you gave was not returned?

Now ask yourself again: Who am I hurting today? What is this anger inside me? How is it fuelled by the way I live? Is my tongue an instrument of peace?

Lust

You can lust after anything and anyone, not simply the objects of your sexual desire. In fact sexual desire may be the easiest lust to give up. The Buddhist monk, Venerable Ajahn Sumedho recorded in his narratives of monastic life that when he was a young novice food was highly restricted but one thing allowed was sugar:

> So then I found myself having a fantastic obsession
> with sweets while before I had not really cared about
> sweets at all. When word got around that we'd have
> cocoa, one could not think about anything else. I did
> not find sexual desire any problem in those days,
> because my obsessions were with sugar and sweets.
> I'd go to bed at night and dream about pastry shops.

Knowing your anger

Write down:

1. The things that make you angry – situations, objects, events, people.

2. People who always make you feel angry and fed-up.

3. How they do that.

4. Are any of these faults also true of you sometimes?

5. Has your anger ever really changed anything or anybody?

Knowing your lust

Write down:

1. The things or situations that other people have which you envy.

2. How having these yourself would change your life.

3. How these changes would help you to love more.

Lust underpins all obsessions and employs a full-time scout for more of the same. This scout is Envy who is always searching for things we might lust after. These obsessions occupy our inner space so much that we forget the spiritual values that keep us focused on the eternal.

Over-consumption

Over-consumption is a formidable hindrance to the spiritual life. As well as overeating and over-drinking, over-consumption is also about indulging ourselves with other things so much that we lose all sense of satiety for other important aspects of living. Over-consumption in any form fills us up and gives us a spiritual bellyache. More is OK as long as it does not in itself become a way of life. By nature we are consumers, but our appetites do not have to be blindly voracious. This dulls our sense of personal identity and we wind up using some standard for living which is a passing human fashion rather than one based on values that reflect the spiritual. For example, our enormous waste of natural resources in the pursuit of unnecessary shopping disregards the inherent gifts of Mother Earth; the intrusion of our tourism simply for holiday novelty cares nothing for the unwelcome changes it may bring others. If instead we respect natural resources we will also respect nature which is a realm of God; if we cultivate awareness and regard for other cultures we will gain understanding which is a foundation for love.

Quick over-consumption test

1. Do you have a compulsion to go shopping?
2. Do you buy lots of gifts for others to show them how you feel?
3. Do you eat as if food was simply fuel? Is it only a quick fix of energy that will keep you going?
4. Do you think you have a right to enjoy life?
5. Do you worry all the time about getting ahead?
6. Do you have a wardrobe full of clothes you never wear?
7. Do you think keeping up with the neighbours is OK?

If you answered yes to
Question 1: go no further. Stop now – you have got a bad case of over-consumption.
Question 2: *things* do not tell people how you feel inside yourself. The lover who gives a bouquet of roses is much appreciated, but when did flowers ever replace the words: 'I love you', spoken from the heart.
Question 3: Food is more than energy to keep life going. It is symbolic of life and an expression of love: we cannot live without food and preparing and serving it to others, or eat-

Of all our urges to consume to excess, our impulse to eat is one of the best understood in terms of our behaviour, physiology and evolution. Our biological mechanisms, designed to respond to adequate food intake by causing us to stop eating, are highly developed. They are also very complex, in that there are a number of different ways for your body to create an individual 'stop eating' signal, and this frequently seems to fail. Various factors override our feeling of satiety and we overeat.

One of these factors is our taste for variety in food. Studies show that given a single-flavoured diet, a rat regulates its body weight, but if artificial flavours are added to the same diet to cre-

---

ing together is a unifying force between people and helps forge strong bonds of affection and understanding.

Question 4: If you think you have a *right* to a happy life you have an overblown sense of self-entitlement. You are in deep trouble, because those who claim such a right often show little concern for others and a lot of resentment if they don't get what they want. We may all deserve happiness, but God is not going to automatically supply it – we have to make an effort too.

Question 5: A continual feeling that you must work to get ahead of others in the social and work scenes of your life is a sign of discontent with what you have and who you are.

Question 6: Why have a wardrobe full of anything that you never use? Hoarding can be a symptom of anxiety. You are suffering from Classic Consumption Gluttony.

Question 7: As to keeping up with your neighbours and colleagues at work, ask yourself if they really care. If not why should you? You are suffering from a compulsion to overspend on goods and services you probably do not need and may not even really want. Are you really that insecure about whether you love yourself?

ate four varieties of taste the rat increases its intake – in some cases to more than twice as much as normal. The food industry has long been aware of this response to variety in food. Next time you go to the supermarket just note the number of flavours of any *one* food they sell – for example, how many variations on plain apple sauce there are for babies. So variation in flavour means more eating.

Social factors also play a important part in overeating. Seeing another animal eat creates the desire to eat more after normal satiety in many animals. This social evidently enhances false hunger signals in the body. The more we eat together, the more we overeat. Think of dinner parties. Think of a big table loaded with food. Think of a fast food restaurant with all those people eating. Another factor that causes us to miss the signal to stop eating is stress. Repeated laboratory tests have shown that animals increase their food intake to abnormal levels when exposed to stress. So when people get anxious or depressed they may overeat.

Such overeating is only a quick fix and no cure. You are trying to run away from your feelings by the activity of eating. This doesn't work because you need to discover what is causing your anxiety and depression. Facing up to the reality of the state you are in and not substituting something else, like eating, is to begin the process of understanding. Such understanding is part of loving yourself. If you must indulge in some substitution, then try listening to music, going for a walk or visiting a friend – some gentle activity that does not hurt you in any way. If you need professional help to find the source of your anxiety or depression, then seek it so that your treatment becomes part of your process of self-acceptance.

When we pursue our goals with a persistence born of our inherent opportunistic human nature we are guilty of spiritual gluttony. In the West we are constantly confronted with opportunities. We do not just overeat, we over-shop, over-sleep and over-entertain ourselves; we overburden ourselves by the sheer volume of our realised opportunities. Most of us live a life in which opportunities to satisfy our passing whims and fancies are the very definition of our society. The result is a flowering of self-indulgence. We live in a culture of entitlement, where we are encouraged to believe we have a *right* to whatever we want. This has given us a false sense of our own superiority. It allows us to rationalise and suppress many outwards signs of our greed. It is not surprising that in the richest nation of all, the United States, those who can most gratify this sense of entitlement are today looking for some spiritual dimension to restore balance in their life of plenty. They are seeking to make some kind of moral restitution to minimise their growing awareness of their greed and over-abundance of comforts. This awareness usually comes in the form of the uneasy question: 'Is this all there is to life?'

Superabundance of material possessions can ruin the most spiritual of people. Saints and mystics avoid it because it can reduce a person's life to a chaos of desires which are never satisfied. We can be spoiled by privilege. Sadly, we teach our children to over-consume and over-value material possessions. Having destroyed their sense of proportion, discouraged them from learning that having more will not bring them lasting happiness, and created in them an overweening self-centredness, we claim to be shocked when they care for nothing, including themselves. The responsibility for this is a collective one. We all share in making life a *nothingness* by our substitution of privileges, entitlements, self-indulgence and material things for the love of our true self and others.

We live in the Age of Substitution and a time of profound waste. The reality of such substituition is that it cannot replace the true expressions of our self, including our creative gifts. Such waste is spiritual as well as material.

Escaping from over-consumption and self-indulgence

Throughout the history of spirituality, men and women have chosen to perform an act of self-denial to surmount the demands of their senses and ego. Many people today think self-denial means you are not loving yourself, because we have come to equate self-indulgence with such love. But it is not loving yourself to over-consume and to burden yourself with the conflicts and frustrations of many desires. Even a little victory over these aspects in your life will give you a chance to express how you *really* feel, and this is an act of love.

Here are two exercises in self-denial that are positive ways to love yourself. The first has to do with raising your awareness of the precious gift of food and helping you to reflect on how you treat it – is it just fuel, or a substitute, or an indulgence without real meaning? The second is to help you exercise a personal power which does not depend on money or possessions and which lets you see that you need not be ruled by your desires. These are gentle ways to help you to understand something more about yourself for spiritual reasons. The paradox of this kind of self-denial is that it can arouse your spiritual awareness (which is an act of love) even though to begin with it may seem like self-inflicted punishment.

Develop a positive relationship with yourself

In a spiritual sense self-affirmation is the sister of self-denial. It is a positive and pleasant way to loving yourself which is based on finding out just how nice you are. It is an even more powerful spiritual tool than denial. We need to acclaim those good aspects of ourselves which are our strengths even more than our failings, because the more we are conscious of the good in ourselves the more likely we are to make this what we show to other people. For

1. Experiencing hunger

Few people today in the powerful developed countries ever experience a real sense of hunger. Even tramps begging on the streets usually can turn to some hand-out of food, no matter how scant. Can you recall feeling hungry? What was it like? Did your belly draw in and feel achy? Do this exercise as a reminder of the importance of food. *Drink a lot of water over these four days, but no coffee, tea or alcohol. Do not smoke. If you are pregnant, do not do this exercise.*

Day 1.Eat breakfast and dinner but no lunch

Day 2.Eat breakfast and a cup of soup for dinner.

Day 3.Eat breakfast and for the rest of the day take only pure water.

Day 4.Repeat Day 3.

Day 5.Get up hungry. Let yourself feel hunger. Write down what it feels like to you. Eat a light supper in the evening and resume your normal intake of food.

2. Purchase avoidance

We have been led to believe that shopping empowers people. This is great sales psychology. But to be able to afford something you like and not buy it is a real power-lift. This is called *purchase avoidance*. It unchains your heart from all those unnecessary desires for things. It is the exact opposite of society's view that consumption is always OK and the more, the better. You will have fun doing this – it is an amazing game in self-control and personal power. You can win!

Day 1. Go to town and window-shop. Do not go in the shops.

Day 2. Go to town and look around in the shops.

Day 3. Go to town, look in the shops for something you really would like to own and can afford to buy. Find it but do not buy it.

Days 4 and 5. Repeat Day 3.

example, if I discover that I have a great capacity for patience when I'm following cooking recipes, I may apply that same patience to other situations – perhaps I will be more tolerant of a work colleague or look more kindly on the self-made problems of a friend. Developing this talent for patience as a loving aspect of myself is to give it a spiritual dimension.

Develop a positive relationship with yourself

Here are some things you can do to help develop this new relationship with your true self:

1. Write down at least ten things you really like about yourself. Reflect on what these say about you.

2. Ask your best friends why they like you. This can be a mirror in which you discover why you deserve love. Write them down.

3. The next time someone acknowledges the good in you, do not be embarrassed or turn the compliment away – take it into your inner space, see it as a real part of you, and love yourself for it.

4. Treat one day as a special for yourself (not your birthday or another day when you would be celebrating in any case). For this one day do exactly what you want. Give yourself time in which to feel good deep inside yourself.

5. The next time you make a mistake, don't dwell on it and fill yourself with self-criticism. Instead, take it as a lesson, resolve to do better next time, then reward yourself for having learned something.

The blocks that can bar our way through the Gateway of Loving can be many and formidable. Here are some of the most common challenges that you may wish to tackle if they are blocking your way to loving yourself.

A lack of trust in yourself

We often deny our gut feelings about something, but intuition is part of us. It is a deep inner awareness that may differ a lot from what we at first perceive in a situation that confronts us. Learn to trust your feelings in such a case.

Do not regard yourself lightly or mock how you really feel. You are part of God and that makes the *whole* of you very special. Learn to have a high but honest respect for yourself and this will help you to respect others. For example, if you feel like crying, then cry and don't regard yourself as weak or a sissy; or if your heart goes out to a stranger who is suffering, do not think of yourself as sentimental but rather as compassionate.

Guilt

Guilt is a huge block to self-love and most of us suffer a lot from guilty feelings. It's important to remember that loving others does not mean you take responsibility for their actions. For example, if you have a partner who is an alcoholic, their drinking is *not* your problem and you have no reason to feel guilty about it. Perhaps you have an elderly mother who knows she should be in a nursing home but refuses to go. You do not need to feel guilty every time she falls down and you are not there. The list of what we can feel guilty about is really endless – even little things like eating too many chocolates can fill us with momentary remorse. All this feeling guilty is simply a way of not accepting our true self. In the examples I gave above, accepting the addiction of a partner as not your problem means you can get on with making your own life right, which may be the most loving thing you can do not just for yourself but also for your partner. In the case of the elderly mother, if you have done all you can to secure her safety and comfort, then you need to respect her right to determine the conditions of her own life, and to accept you have done your best. As to eating too many chocolates, if you share them that should remove any feeling of guilt.

Fear

Fears are a natural aspect of being human and we all have them from time to time. I think the best way to handle fear is to face what it is you fear and find out why. The better you understand fear the more you can deal with it. Feeling guilty does nothing to diminish fear or face it, and means you are refusing to accept part of yourself. The next time you fear something, write down what it is and think about what holding on to it means in your life. If it was not there, would you be happier? If it remains a threat, will it ever happen? Would you feel stronger and more content if you defeated it?

A belief that we are separate individuals and somehow not connected to others

Since God includes everyone and everything, it means you are intimately connected to all other life. The more you accept your true self, the more your awareness of this holy connection will grow. This means that you belong not just to yourself but to every-body else. Our sense of wholeness depends on this vision. If you want to make your individuality shine, acknowledging how you really feel and living out these truths will connect you not just to yourself but to others.

A belief that we are right and the other person is wrong or that we are always wrong and that others are always right

Nobody likes somebody who always feels they are right. Equally, you cannot be wrong all the time. Since you are perfect in God alone, you are going to be right sometimes and wrong sometimes in this life. Accepting that natural condition is part of loving your-self. So next time you want to argue about being right, let the other person have an easy victory for a change. If you are always feeling that you are wrong, ask yourself why you should persist in this impossibility.

The key of forgiveness

Show me a person who does not need to be forgiven and I will know he is dead. We cannot live without hurting others either by intention or by accident and the act of begging forgiveness begins inside us. First we need to acknowledge what we have done and forgive ourselves for our failure. Since God who is within knows all we do, he hears our confession too. From this reconciliation we can go forward with honesty to the person we have hurt and ask forgiveness through the apology of the opened heart. It is a matter of putting our spiritual life back in order. First with ourselves and God, and then with others. This means we must also forgive those who have hurt us. Reconciliation is the wisdom of forgiveness and it opens the heart to love.

Pairing and parting

Most couples manage to settle down together. Shared joys and crises are part of an intimate relationship. We read a lot about the divorce rate, and even if we are still with our original partner, we know someone who is on marriage number two or yet another relationship that 'this time is different'. Today pairing up and parting in a hurry is the fashion although making commitments seems increasingly difficult for people, especially men. Such frequent pairing and parting gives us a sense of failure and rejection. It makes us angry too. These are grave hindrances to our well-being and spiritual life.

But have we failed? Have we not managed to love enough? Have we been too self-centred? Did our partner not match up to our expectations? We ask ourselves such questions again and again and none of the answers ever seem to make the next relationship any better. One main reason is that we demand such close relationships today that it is almost an invitation to failure. A healthy relationship is one in which two people are deeply involved with each other but reserve enough time and space for other relationships and interests. This allows each person enough time in the sanctuary of their inner space. We need to learn to live as a guest in the other person's sense of personal space. If you cry out 'Give me space!' then you are overdue for a visit to your interior realm. And if you are in need of time in inner space, so is your partner.

Loving lies in allowing each other time for an interior life where another relationship takes place between the self and God. If this relationship, which is based in love, is strong and nourished by the way you live, then all your other relationships are more likely to be fortified by the understanding that comes from love.

Smiling: the heart's greeting

Showing friendliness to other people is an easy way to get yourself started in the process of loving. It does not have to be some generous or thoughtful act: you can start with a smile – not one plastered on your face but one which comes straight from your heart because you feel that way.

When shown slides of smiling people, American students in a recent study rated the most attractive models in the photographs as those who smiled and expressed an open body position – that is without crossing their legs or folding their arms. Smiling and other body language frequently communicate more truth about how we feel than our words. There are lots of different kinds of smiles, from shy ones to loving ones. In fact we are filled up with smiles waiting to be used. There are smiles for every occasion and, most importantly, for no special occasion. That's the smile you give to a stranger just because the day is nice, the sunshine good on your face, or you are glad to be alive and want to share that feeling. Your smile says it all.

Our smiling brings its own reward, for it changes us physically and psychologically for the better. The more you smile, the more likely you are to have good emotional health. It has long been said that laughter is the best medicine: perhaps all healing starts with a smile. Smiling is full of hope and hope works miracles. Today, to brighten up your soul, try smiling at everyone you meet.

Hugging: reconnecting to your body.

Hugging is good for you. It is an investment in love. When a friend or a partner is sad or has a problem, why always try to give them words? The next time, shut up and give them a hug instead. It can heal. It is an embrace of the spirit. It expresses how you feel deep inside. It works.

Here are three hugging exercises. Before you begin remember these guidelines to hugging: a hug must be given out of genuine feeling; don't try to hug people who prefer to have some space; and don't make the other person embarrassed or uncomfortable.

Hugging Practice

The self-hug
Wrap your arms around yourself, grabbing each upper arm with the opposite hand. Left hand, right arm. Right hand, left arm. Now squeeze hard, giving yourself a big hug.

Hugging 1
Pick a time at home when there seems to be no conflict or arguments going on. Say to your partner or a friend: 'I need to give you a hug.' Most people will not refuse you. Put both your arms around the person and give them a big hug. Now thank them, looking straight into their eyes.

Hugging 2
Do the same thing as above only say: 'You need a hug.'

Solitude and loving: balancing intimacy and independence

From time to time we all have a desire for solitude as a means of escape from the pressures and stresses of ordinary life. A desire for solitude does not mean you are unhappy or that you do not have successful relationships. Our Western culture makes the peace of solitude a rare commodity, hard to attain. This is one reason why the spiritual retreat movement has grown so much in the last twenty years.

If we are to know ourselves in order to love, we must have a degree of solitude in our lives – a chance to be alone and regain a sense of personal space. In this inner space, we can come to a better understanding about ourselves, which can put some sense of wholeness back into our life when it gets too fragmented. In inner space we may discover our illusions and admit our errors. Solitude is a preparation for listening to God.

The desire to be alone is not always acceptable to others. They think if someone wants to be alone and away from their closest friends, partner or family, that somehow that person is not being loving. Nothing could be further from the truth, for having some space in which to be ourselves makes for better relationships.

Psychologists, psychoanalysts, geneticists, anthropologists, biologists and other investigators of our humanity have differing views on our need for solitude and its opposite, intimacy. For most of us it is enough to recognise that these needs exist and to incorporate them into the way we live out our life. The problems arise when an individual does not recognise this and either remains too much in solitude without closeness to others or puts all their efforts into being close to others. Without a balance we end up in a life where there is no silence or space in which to hear the interior voice of the self. Without this we can develop conflicts and stresses which may lead not only to failed relationships but to disease, deep unhappiness and even madness. As the poet, W.B.

Yeats, wrote, 'Things fall apart, the centre cannot hold.'

Few creatures in the animal kingdom are monogamous and for those that are, like the gibbon, it is hard to distinguish between the genders. Marked sexual difference in humans seem to indicate that we have attention-seeking differences, such as female breasts, intended to attract in a society where partners are often changed. We are told by researchers that human males look for many partners to spread around their genes and that women too are genetically inclined to stray, but tend to monogamy since someone must bring up the children. If this genetic picture is right, then it is not surprising that the comparatively recent convention of marriage puts a huge strain on most men and woman. It too, of course, has a genetic function, for it gives some stability to the long period of child-rearing that humans require. So we persist in having marriage or a similar long-term partnership as a goal. It seems most of us want a one-to-one stable relationship whether or not we intend to have children, in spite of what the researchers tell us or the high rate of divorce and separation.

A high percentage of people still manage to beat the odds and remain faithful to their partner, be a good parent, and live out a life together. This encourages everyone else to keep trying. But there has been a growing demand and expectation for such a relationship to be one of increasing closeness so that intimacy itself makes for a kind of claustrophobia. We become stressed from this lack of personal space, but keep trying all sorts of techniques and schemes to improve our relationship except the one which might actually have the greatest effect – a bit of being alone. Some soul time. This drive for ever greater intimacy without the balancing aspect of solitude does not take us any closer to the other person and is a hindrance to love. Our inner space is invaded and taken over by our relationship. Everybody suffers.

Heart space: making room for love

If you base all your love on *physical* closeness with other people and believe this to be the definition of intimacy, then you will soon find that moods take over the relationship. Moments of silence and solitude are essential for love to flourish. You need to give the opportunity for silence and solitude both to yourself and the other person. This is also true for the relationship between parent and child. You can then both experience the personal freedom to be yourself. One of the relationship problems for many people when they retire arises from the fact that suddenly both partners are at home together after years of work and domestic routines that previously gave each of them enough personal space. The shed at the bottom of the garden or the garage workshop is a classic refuge for a man, while going out shopping becomes a solution for many women. Golf courses are littered with non-sporting types who took up the game just to *get away*. In most cases there may not be much wrong with the relationship save too much intimacy and not enough solitude for inner-space time. Getting away from it all once in a while is a love-saver.

Our instinct is to be together with someone and at the same time to be free of them. This is natural. It does not need to be the source of conflict if you accept that both of you have a profound need for the intimacy of love with another human and an equally deep yearning for the freedom to be your true self. This freedom belongs to the spirit and involves the most intimate of all our relationships, which is between the self and God. Our intimacies are made both of earthly love and spiritual love and their essences are not different. These loves form the two parts of the same inseparable heart, for all human love subsists through God's love.

What does your heart say? What do you feel for that other person in your life. Admiration? Gratitude? Affection? Passion? Look inside yourself and let how you really feel be the way you love. Your love will be true because it comes from within.

Assessing your primary relationship

Ask these questions of your current relationship and then think about your answers. What do they tell you about the reality of your intimacy? What do they tell you about yourself? What about the other person in your life?

1. Can you handle it when your partner wants to be left alone? What do you say and do?
2. Do you behave with your partner as if the two of you were *one* person?
3. Does one of you try to dictate how the other should behave?
4. Are things going the way you both want them to?
5. Are things going the way that suits each of you as individuals?
6. Do you expect the other person to take care of your needs?
7. Do you believe your happiness depends on your partner? Why?

The lover and the beloved

When I was a little boy my grandmother told me that there were two kinds of people in the world. One kind was called *the lover* and the other *the beloved*. She was certain that we were born with a destiny to be one or the other of these in all our intimate relationships. I think we need to be both kinds of person, because to exist in a state of love means we have to both give it and receive it. This makes the heart whole and God rejoices, for love is the ground of our being. What about you? Have you always seemed to be the lover or are you the beloved of someone? What does it mean to be a lover then? What does it mean to be the beloved?

We might think that the lover has all the problems of pursuit, courtship, wooing, keeping fidelity going, making the amends that heal: taking the initiative of love in all its little and grand forms. For the beloved in such a case there can be a heavy burden lurking in all this attention. To be adored too much is to be worshipped, and this is a burden for the soul. If someone tells you that you are the anchor in their life, do not take this as a compliment. Each of us needs to be anchored in God and this means to be anchored in our true self.

Which are you?

1. Decide if you are the lover or the beloved.

2. Write down three things that make you think that.

3. Now if you were the other one, what would be three things that define you?

The art of loving

> I will not look for perfection in another person until
> I have attained perfection for myself. Since I know
> this will never be, let me learn to accept things as
> they are, and stop manipulating them into changing.
> Let me look for a wiser approach to life from myself,
> not from other people.
>
> Al-Anon: 'One Day at a Time'

If there is a secret to the art of loving, surely it must lie in letting the other person be themselves and not trying to change them. This sensitivity should prompt the way you act towards the other person, for the goal of intimacy is a closeness that does not smother the inner space of either person.

St Francis of Sales (1567–1622) remains famous for his work of spiritual direction, *Introduction to the Devout Life*, but he also composed many letters to friends and followers. In one of these he wrote:

Those who are filled with an earthly love are always thinking of the object of their attachment, their heart brims with affection for it, their mouth is always full of its praise. When absent, they constantly speak of their love in letters, engrave the treasured name on every tree. In the same way those who love God are never tired of thinking of him, living for him, seeking him and talking to him.

If you want to live a sacred life then you want to be this second kind of person, the one who makes God stay in consciousness and does not allow the sacred to slip back into the hidden. You want the spirit right up front in your life.

Love potions

During this next week try these prescriptions for helping love to grow in your life

1. Close your eyes. It's party time in your heart. Who would you invite? What would you tell them of your love? Act on these feelings so that the person you love will know how much you care.

2. How can you know compassion if you are always finding fault with yourself? Start being able to love more by loving yourself first. Just as you really are. Make a list of all your good points and study it the next time you catch yourself indulging in self-criticism.

3. Your capacity for love should grow bigger all your life. It thrives best if you love people as they are with all their faults and failings. Generosity and understanding are the food of love. Make a list of all the good aspects of your partner or a close friend. Remember them the next time they irritate or anger you.

Inscribed above the Gateway of Loving are these holy words
which you must place forever in your heart:

'You must love the Lord God with all your heart,
with all your soul, with all your mind and with all
your strength. You must love your neighbour as you
love yourself.'

(Mark 12:30–31)

THE SIXTH GATEWAY

Celebration – The way of belonging to Creation

Father eternal, Mother all-loving,

Spirit most holy, friend to all Creation,

yours be glory, praise and adoration.

(Based on a ninth-century monastic hymn)

There is an old saying that life itself is a celebration, and I believe we should make this true for ourselves because there can be nothing more exciting than just the simple fact of being alive. The more we are aware of this, the more we discover that the mystery of life is matched by the wonder of how it all interconnects. Then we realise that the universe is one marvellous and continuous whole and that we are part of it. Once we understand that we are not separate from the Creation, our understanding draws us nearer to God, who contains all things. To understand and rejoice in this is a celebration that takes us into the garden of the soul.

If current scientific theories are correct, the universe will never collapse on itself. It appears to exist in a kind of balancing act between potential collapse and infinite expansion. The universe, in other words, is skateboarding through eternity – just coasting along for ever, in a state of continuous change. What a truly grand cosmic adventure we are on – because as part of that universe we are also constantly changing, continually forming, unfolding, altering, and *becoming*.

But what is the essential aspect of ourselves that could be continuously expanding in keeping with this universal nature? Since our bodies and minds have limitations, perhaps it is our spiritual selves which are continually expanding and, thus, perhaps our spirituality is driven by the very force and nature of the universe itself. Could this explain our spiritual hunger, our religious beliefs, our need to find meaning to life, and our deep yearning to be conscious of the mysterious eternal? Is this why we seek the perfection of the cosmos, the enlightenment of the Buddha, and the presence of the risen Christ? Is our existence meant to be a journey of the soul to union with God; is it this that defines what it is to be a human? If these things are true, then we exist in a universe that is not in turmoil. On the contrary, we exist in a universe whose nature is to be always unfolding and creating. Thus, we live in a state of true genesis, of being *born* – and what could be more joyous to celebrate than a birth, because this is new life, and that new life is your own.

So then this is what we should all declare in celebration of being alive: *As I reach out, so God reaches out to me. I am like the universe, endlessly unfolding, infinitely expanding, but always contained within the cosmic embrace. The garden of my soul is a circle reflecting this unending nature.*

Connecting to the universal centre

A circle which has neither beginning nor end is a traditional spiritual way to see the oneness of creation. The idea that there is at the centre of the circle a core hub or navel which corresponds to the universe and that all Creation comes from this divine centre is also an ancient belief, still much in evidence around the world today. The ancient Greeks called this notion *omphalos*. For Buddhists it is Mount Meru. For Christians it may be the Garden of Eden. In all religions there is this idea of a centre, an *axis mundi*, from which radiates all Creation. It is illustrated by the circle, which is the shape of infinity: an endless but continuing line where the beginning is invisible and there is no ending. Here is the concept of the expanding universe, the cosmos which is continuous, holding all life together and within itself. For this reason the circle is one of the most powerful signs of the spiritual and can be used to enter the Gateway of Celebration. It represents divine powers. So contemplating my navel would not be a waste of time if, as for a yogi, such meditation led me to centre on my inner space which is where my consciousness of Creation starts.

Here is the revelation of the sacred circle as experienced by Black Elk (1863–1950), a Native American mystic of the Oglala Sioux:

> Then I was standing on the highest mountain of them all, and round about beneath me was the whole hoop of the world. And while I stood there I saw more than I can tell and I understood more than I saw; for I was seeing in a sacred manner the shapes of all things in the spirit, and the shape of all shapes as they must live together like one being. And I say the sacred hoop of my people was one of the many hoops that made one circle, wide as daylight and as starlight, and in the centre grew one mighty flowering tree to shelter all the children of one mother and one father. And I saw that it was holy . . . But anywhere is the centre of the world.

Creating a spiritual circle

We can use the circle to focus our inner self and to increase our spiritual awareness. Native Americans as part of shamanic spiritual practise have traditionally made a circle or hoop, often called a medicine wheel, to prepare themselves for entering into consciousness of Creation. It is a centring that brings them into the spiritual realm with time and space aligned to the four earth directions of north, south, east and west. Each direction is a realm of spiritual power. North is white like snow and is the realm of wisdom. South is where you find purity of heart. East is yellow like the sun and is a place of illumination. In the west, where the wind blows off the wide seas you will find the powers of prayer and reflection. The Medicine Wheel, even for people separated from a shared ritual in a culture of which you are a member, still remains a way of centring yourself and of calling into consciousness the true *axis mundi* of self. It takes you to a place that is a starting point for celebrating Creation: it is a vehicle for taking you through the Gateway of Celebration.

Building a medicine wheel

The building of a medicine wheel should be an act of the spirit, an offering of thanksgiving to Creation, and a calling forth of the spiritual. The making of a medicine wheel is in itself a form of prayer like the painting of icons in Eastern Orthodox Christianity. Make it a ritual of contemplation, offering, and spiritual unfolding. If creating the medicine wheel centres you in stillness and your inner self, this can bring reverence, which is a perception of God by the soul.

1. Collect two piles of stones: you will need 32 altogether – 8 small ones and 24 large ones.
2. You can build your wheel on a table or on the floor, but it's best if you can build it outside on the ground because this

connects you directly with the earth. Go barefoot if you can.

3. Find out where north, south, east and west lie. Sit facing south, which is the direction of purity of heart and a good place to begin all sacred journeys. You might like to use a mantra to take you into stillness and a state of innocence:

> Lord of Creation, give me a pure heart.
>
> Lord of Creation, give me a pure heart.
>
> Lord of Creation, give me a pure heart.

4. Close your eyes and begin your travel into inner space. Repeat the mantra, 'Lord of Creation, give me a pure heart', until you are still and at peace. Now visualise two circles, one inside the other.

5. Keeping yourself in this state of stillness, and remaining in your interior realm, slowly open your eyes.

6. Begin to make a circle with twelve of the large stones. There should be one at each of the four directions, with two in between each direction. As you place each stone, concentrate on it. Look at its shape, colour, shadow and light. See with the eyes of your heart the wonder of its stillness. Feel its presence on earth.

7. Make another circle inside the larger one with the eight small stones, concentrating on each of them in the same way.

8. Now connect the outer circle with the inner one. Placing three large stones to connect the inner circle to the outer circle at each direction. You will have formed the shape of a wheel with an outer rim and spokes that lead from it to a central hub.

9. Now place something to represent the powers of each direction just outside the circle. For example, you might put a yellow leaf or a flower in the north to symbolise the

power of illumination. As you place each symbolic object,
let your inner eye travel in that direction. Leave your
mind open, free, and unattached to desires. Meditate on
each object you place – the colour of the leaf or flower, the
surface of the stone, the smoothness of the shell – see in
each the nature of itself.

The centre of your circle is an outward reflection of an interior
centre – the heart of your spiritual realm. When you enter this
realm, what does your heart see? What things of earth will greet
you? What wonderful visions present themselves? What sights
from memory are stirred? What is the oasis of peace beyond the
changing sands of your life? Recall that you have made this journey in celebration of life and in the yearning to reconnect yourself
to the universal source of Creation.

You have arrived at the navel of the world, unlocking inner
energies and expanding consciousness from the visible part of
Creation into the invisible cosmos. In this way you have become
the cosmos itself, the ever changing, the everlasting. Here is the
ancient shamanic place where all spirits live, a realm of healing
and transformation. It is a place of the pure heart, a holy ground
of being and a meeting place with God, creator of your spirit,
which having neither beginning nor ending knows no death.

You can leave the medicine wheel after this first meditation
and return it whenever you want to centre yourself again. If you
need to dismantle it, do so slowly and with respect. As you take
each element away, study its form. Let your thoughts be small
meditations on your relationship to all other things.

The shamanic vision of Creation

Many native peoples around the world still maintain an essentially shamanic vision of reality and the universe: they see all life as one. This vision comes from their shamanic journeys into altered states of consciousness where they *see* the spiritual realm. The following is how Edmund Nequatewa, a Native American Hopi, expressed this vision. It is not only *inclusive* of all external and interior realities, but is a belief in the unity of all life.

> To the Hopi all life is one – it is the same. This world where he lives is the human world and in it all the animals, birds, insects, and every living creature, as well as the trees and plants which also have life, appear only in masquerade, or in forms in which we ordinarily see them. But it is said that all these creatures and these living things that share the spark of life with us humans, surely have other homes where they live in human forms like ourselves. Therefore, all these living things are thought of as humans and they may sometimes be seen in their own forms even on earth. If they are killed, then the soul of this creature may return to its own world which it may never leave again, but the descendants of this creature will take its place in the human world, generation after generation.
>
> (*The Book of the Hopi*)

What can be the meaning of '... where they live in human forms like ourselves' except to suggest that all creatures are spiritual like ourselves and in this spiritual form we are alike. All forms of life are united in this common spiritual identity, and can recognise that together they belong to God. When Edmund Nequatewa says, 'then the soul of this creature may return to its own world which it may never leave again', what is this but an expression of the return of each form of life to its Creator?

The importance of the idea of a Creator is not so much to endorse any particular creation mythology or belief, but to affirm the transcendence and lordship of the Absolute to which we belong and to which the soul returns. By calling God the Creator of everything that constitutes life as we know it, we can celebrate this universal oneness by focusing on God as the power core of the eternal circle. Devotees of Vishnu, the largest group of mainstream Hindus, believe God exhibits six ultimate qualities: knowledge, strength, lordship, heroism, power and splendour. In the Book of Revelation 1:8, John sees the Eternal One sitting on the throne, who says to him: 'I am the Alpha and the Omega' – the Beginning and the End.

Since everything seen and unseen is within God, and since everything is God, we cannot be a separate entity apart from God. So we are part of the beginning and the ending and of the centre of all knowledge, strength, lordship, heroism, power and splendour. This gives us great cause to celebrate. We can do that by raising our awareness of the presence of the Creator God in the creatures around us and the earth on which we live. Our souls can sing out in gladness at the splendour.

God in his creatures

We persist in believing that our pets and other animals share an emotional life similar to our own: a life that involves happiness, sadness, depression, joy, loyalty, humour and all the many aspects of behaviour that we recognise as human feelings. We say our dog *smiles* at us or that our cat is *happy* when curled up in our lap. It has long been considered unscientific to ascribe human charac-

teristics to non-human beings in this manner. But lately a growing number of respected investigators have admitted to sharing
these widely held and popular sentiments, although they may still
try not to use words which attribute human feelings to other forms
of life when they write up their research. As such scientists
become familiar with the subject of their investigation, whether
it be an ape or a rabbit, they privately express their wonder in emotional words just like the rest of us – words like *joy* and *sorrow*. The
more we make friends with other living creatures, the more aware
we are of how we treat them. To be against the factory farming of
chickens is not to romanticise every chicken into a cute little hen,
but to make a moral judgement that something is wrong with
being so cruel to them. When people discover that plant-eating
cows are being fed ground up animals, many feel disgust at an
activity which seems to them 'against nature'.

We cannot rid ourselves of the feeling that we somehow share
a life with other creatures and that there is a right and a wrong way
to live with them, even if we do eat some of them. Salmonella poi-
soning from chickens and the advent of mad cow disease have
served to heighten this awareness even at political levels. Who
knows what unhappy surprises may await us from genetically
altered food crops or from the effect of chemicals in the food
chain? Who is to decide the ethical and moral issues raised by the
creation of cloned and transgenic creatures? The degree of kinship
between all forms of life gets more mysterious as our scientific
knowledge grows, not less. We need to lift our current awareness
into a vision of life that makes how we treat it a real celebration
of the holy. This is to take on board our sacred responsibility to act
like we are part of Creation and not just a consumer of it.

Interpreting the behaviour of the animals around us in terms
of human experience and values does not demean their uniqueness. How else are we to understand our oneness with them in this
world? We accept today that our pets can help us feel less lonely.
We know that stroking a cat may lower our blood pressure. Where

nothing else seems to work with a disturbed child, an animal may do wonders. When someone says that her best relationship is with her dog, it may be a more positive and healthy relationship than many between humans.

If it helps us to live more joyfully and in harmony with nature to believe that a cat dreams 'happily' in the sunshine, a dog is 'loyal', a nightingale 'adores' singing, that an elephant 'mourns', and that a horse may 'fall in love', then why not? Perhaps it is a way of reflecting on what it means in our own lives when we too have such feelings of happiness, loyalty, adoration, mourning or joy. Could there be a better way to profess your deeply private communion with all other creatures than through the under-standing of your own humanity when held up to the mirror of their natures?

I believe that what we feel about other creatures reflects how we feel about ourselves and each other. It is this personal vision, not their reality, which can help us develop our spiritual life. They are a living presence through which we may discover more about ourselves and deepen our spiritual life. When I can see beyond superficial appearances to the kinship that exists between myself and another kind of creature, I become aware of the wonder of Creation. This leads my soul back in celebration to God. In the words of St Francis of Assisi: 'It is God whom they are really see-ing, though they see him only in his creatures.'

Meditating on animals

Many characteristics in the animals we see and know are worthy of celebration and can teach us about ourselves. If we apply these lessons to ourselves, they can bring us closer to perfecting our nature within Creation. Here are five animals on which to medi-tate and help lift your awareness of yourself and of the oneness of life. Make each meditation a little celebration of the existence of each animal.

The cat and a lesson in love

Silent and swift, the cat comes and goes of its own accord, an ambivalent symbol of affection and independence. Equally at home guarding the humblest hearth or the palaces of a pharaoh, the cat insists on equality not ownership. Your cat is faithful to itself and asks only that you follow the same truth. Here is the foundation of all loving relationships. Could you be more true to yourself, like the cat?

The monkey and a lesson in humour

The monkey makes us laugh. The monkey is tickling, teasing and swinging for joy just because it is alive. He is being a fool for God and taking the world as it comes. He is living just for this moment and can show us that inside us is a child also waiting to jump out and enjoy life. Do you have a lost child inside who wants to be found and invited out to laugh and play?

The squirrel and a lesson in possessions

The squirrel hides so much that he forgets where he puts it. Are we, like the squirrel, so worried about the future that we forget where our real treasure is? Ownership can be a heavy burden that takes up time, and physical and psychic energies. Ask any millionaire. This is the danger of plenty. True investments should be these – the time and peace to explore your gifts, to grow into a loving person, and to make frequent trips to your inner space to tend the garden of your soul. In this way, you prepare like a squirrel for the winter of life, but the fruits you store up are those of the spirit. These will nourish you for all eternity. What are the possessions of your heart that money cannot buy?

The cow and a lesson in acceptance

As far as we know, the cow does not dream of greater beauty. She does not want to be younger or wiser. She is content with her form and her life. We need a similar acceptance of ourselves, of where we are at the moment, and the age we are at this time. This affirms and celebrates our own place within Creation. We all need, like the cow, an honest vision of ourselves. Do you need to stop being restless and accept where you are in life?

The swan and a lesson in devotion

The swan is famed for its fidelity – often mating for life, then pining away if its partner should die. Symbol of light, the swan personifies feminine grace as it glides through water and masculine strength in its aerial majesty when it flies. It represents a balance of life, and its defining characteristic is devotion. We too contain both the feminine and the masculine. Our flight is the yearning of the soul for union with God and our celebration of Creation shows our devotion. Does your life have fidelity and love for yourself and others?

Our need to belong to Creation

When we become aware of our deep need to belong to Creation we can begin a journey of understanding that helps us celebrate the gift of life and the wonder of Creation. This takes us straight through the Gateway of Celebration into the garden of the soul.

But what pulls us towards and binds us to other living things? The complexity of our relationship to nature and the fascination, beauty and fear we feel for all living organisms is true of all humans and all social groups. An ultimate answer eludes us, but in 1984, Edmund O. Wilson, one of the most distinguished biologists of the twentieth century, suggested that the reason for this might be that 'the urge to affiliate with other forms of life is to some degree innate'. This urge grows from the very beginning of our childhood. It provides us with material for our scientific curiosity, our myths, and our beliefs in magic. The patterns of such real, imaginative

and spiritual relationships and ideas find a constancy of expression
in all cultures across the world. Professor Wilson explains this phenomenon in his book, *In Search of Nature*, by showing the
universality of people's feelings towards the snake and how this
form of nature has been translated into a cultural symbols, including the serpent in the garden of Eden and the symbol we use today
to signify modern medicine. He comments:

> For hundreds of thousands of years, time enough for
> the appropriate genetic changes to occur in the
> brain, poisonous snakes have been a significant
> source of injury and death to human beings. The
> response to the threat is not simply to avoid it, in
> the way that certain berries are recognised as
> poisonous through a process of trial and error. People
> also display the mixture of apprehension and morbid
> fascination characterising the non-human primates.
> They inherit a strong tendency to acquire the
> aversion during early childhood and to add to it
> progressively, like our closest phylogenetic relatives,
> the chimpanzees. The mind then adds a great deal
> more that is distinctively human. It feeds upon the
> emotions to enrich culture. The tendency of the
> serpent to appear suddenly in dreams, its sinuous
> form, and its power and mystery are the natural
> ingredients of myth and religion.

Serpentine forms are found in the Paleolithic stone carvings of
Europe. They are scratched on to the great mammoth teeth found
in Siberia. The plumed serpent, god of morning and night, is a
dominant element in the lost religion of the ancient Aztecs.
Serpents are the emblems of power and ceremony for many
shamans. In this way, we transform nature into our culture so that
the snake of nature becomes the serpent of human legend. Life in

other forms becomes part of us.

Today, most of us do not practise a spirituality where snakes represent spirits, yet the symbolic element of the serpent remains with us. Examples abound from the practical joke of a paper snake to the latest horror movie about giant serpents invading the world. Today, most of us live in cities where snakes are not usually found, but we keep all our ancient sense of fear and loathing. The snake is buried deep in our unconscious. So are all the other creatures and plants of our natural environment, in one way or another. Professor Wilson concludes: 'Although the evidence is far from all in, the brain appears to have kept its old capacities, its channelled quickness. We stay alert and alive in the vanished forest of the world.'

It may be a similar kind of transformation of nature into our lives which will change our perception of it and provide the necessary motivation from which will come our collective efforts to save the biodiversity of life on this planet rather than to destroy it. A quick look around the world at just a few places shows just how extensive our destruction of Creation has been and how desperately we need to celebrate life and not abuse it.

On the positive side, increased awareness of the necessity of biodiversity, widely available information on the ecosystems of earth and our natural surroundings, and disenchantment with so much of what commercial interests and science would have us believe is 'progress', is leading to a growing collective consciousness of the interrelatedness of all existence. And our consciousness is continually being raised about these issues through the media and pressure groups. When poor farmers from India bring their protest to the great cities of the West that they do not need or want genetically engineered crops, they do us all a favour. They help us to reflect on the ways in which we handle our human needs in a world of interrelated nature. The further we live from nature, the more sterile and less satisfying is our human-made environment and the more our sense of nature lies in our minds rather than our hearts. We know about snakes but may never have seen one. We know what corn looks like but we may have no idea how it is grown. Both the snake and the corn grow dim in the our dreams and myths. Even our spirit begins to forget nature, and our urban surroundings may make it harder for us to hold the vision that our world is one living Creation.

The culture of place: the roots that make us

If we are to make our lives a celebration, we must live in harmony with nature. It is helpful if we understand how much the environments where we grew up and where we now live affect us.

When someone speaks of the environment in terms of nature, it seems to me a foreign thing, distinct from anywhere I recognise. What I do have is a sense of place. This present place where I feel the night wind rising cool from the river l'Adour as it flows down from the Pyrenees. That childhood place where I remember the steam ferry leaving for San Francisco. Any place where the cry of the owl brings forth from my heart the voice of my grandfather and the nightingale's song a call to night prayers and sleep. Here in this Creation where I am planted in the present and in the past, in the dying of my flesh and in the living of my spirit, I have my roots; and these for me are deeply rural and grounded in nature. Whatever you are when you are yourself cannot be separated from your place in Creation. This sense of place largely determines your consciousness of all Creation – how you see it and the life in it, and how close you may feel to it.

The urban person has roots grown in a human-made place. This makes it easy to be alienated from nature and to have a sense of place that is defined by human life in the city. Somewhere between the rural person and the urban person, is that twentieth-century phenomenon – the suburban person, who often longs for a nature that is romantic but tidy. The result can be a nostalgia which is not based in reality. Frankly, most of us would like Creation to be comfortable, but since the essence of nature is unpredictability and change, this is not possible.

The question of place

Write down your responses to these questions and use them to meditate on the roots from which you have grown.

1. Are you an urban, rural or suburban person?

2. What is the reality of the place you are in now?

3. What does this mean to you?

4. How does this connect you to other creatures?

5. How does this connect you to nature?

Looking for celebrations

No matter what your roots or your sense of place, the world around you is still part of Creation. You can celebrate whatever you find there. The colour and excitement of busy streets and the delight of the sheer glass walls of a skyscraper at sunset. The embrace of a small house with its familiar and supportive smells and memories. A place where neat rows of tulips bloom with the same beauty as in the far land of their origin. A moment in the sun when the sweat of your garden labours burns into your eyes and you are grounded in the earth. Reverence is born of accepting that we are of earth and knowing we are shaped by the land of our birth. Neither poverty nor great wealth changes this essential inner truth.

When as individuals we are able to discern the kinship of all things, no matter which spiritual path we choose to follow, we have seen into our true humanity. As the Zen tradition teaches, those who see into their true nature in this way are instantaneously initiated into all the mystic teachings. The response of our soul at such a moment of revelation is to offer praise in an outburst of gladness. We can understand then such words as these from a seventeenth-century Japanese Buddhist poem: 'The Moon is the same old moon, the flowers exactly as they were. Yet I've become the thingness of all the things I see.'

Connecting with nature

This is an exercise in learning to listen with your heart to trees, rocks, flowers, or any particular place (it could be where you live, or a spot you come across while out in the country. Sitting comfortably near the object of your attention, be still and relax yourself. Let all thoughts pass from your mind. Begin now to really look at the the tree, rock or flower. What is it form, texture and colour? Hug the tree, hold the rock, bend down to face the flower. Imagine the miracle of their existence. Is this not a mystery and marvel to which you belong too? Do the same meditation in your home, letting all the smells and memories of the place provoke your sense of place. Are these walls not like arms to embrace you? Is this place not part of nature too?

Six songs of celebration

If we are to live a sacred life, it is important to celebrate Creation, because this helps us to be aware of its mystery and wonder. Here are six songs of celebration to use from time to time for meditation, reflection and prayer. To give thanksgiving for your life.

First celebration

Cry out with joy to the Lord, all the earth.
Serve the Lord with gladness.

Come before him, singing for joy.
Know that he, the Lord is God.
He made us, we belong to him,
we are his people, the sheep of his flock..

Go within his gates, giving thanks.
Enter his courts with songs of praise.

Give thanks to him and bless his name.

Indeed, how good is the Lord,
eternal his merciful love.
He is faithful from age to age.

Old Testament, Psalm 100

Second celebration
O You
who has given me eyes
to see the light
that fills my room
give me the inward vision
to behold you in this place.

Chandra Devanesen, twentieth-century Hindu mystic of
India

Third celebration
O Hidden Life, vibrant in every atom
O Hidden Light, shining in every creature,
O Hidden Love, embracing all in Oneness,
May each who feels himself as one with Thee
Know he is therefore one with every other.

Prayer, Annie Besant, feminist and theosophist (1847–1933)

Fourth celebration

I am water. I am the thorn
that catches someone's clothing.

I don't care about marvellous sights!
I only want to be in your presence.

There's nothing to believe.
Only when I quit believing in myself
did I come into this beauty.

I saw your blade and burned my shield!
I flew on six hundred pairs of wings like Gabriel.
But now that I'm here, what do I need wings for?

Day and night I guarded the pearl of my soul.
Now in this ocean of pearling currents,
I've lost track of which was mine.

'A Dove in the Eaves', Rumi, Sufi mystic (1207–73)

Fifth celebration

Praise be to you above, Most High, for all your
creatures,
Especially your Brother Sun who brings us the day
and sheds his light on us;
Lovely is he, and radiant with splendour,
And he speaks to us of you, O Most High.
Praise be to you, my Lord, for Sister Moon and the
Stars
Whom you have set in the heavens, bright, precious
and fair.
Praise be to you, my Lord, for Brother Wind,
For air and cloud, for calm and all weather
By which you sustain life in all your creatures.

Praise be to you, oh Lord, for Sister Water,
Who is useful and humble, precious and pure.
Praise be to you, my Lord, for Brother Fire,
By whom you light the night;
He is fair and merry, mighty and strong.
Praise be to you, my Lord, for our sister Mother
Earth
Who sustains and governs us
And brings forth varied fruits, bright flowers and
plants.
Praise and bless my Lord, and thank and serve him
with great humility.

'Canticle of the Sun', St Francis of Assisi (1181–1226)

Sixth celebration

Grandfather, Great Spirit, once more behold me on
earth and lean to hear my feeble voice. You lived
first, and you are older than all need, older than all
prayer. All things belong to you – the two-legged,
the four-legged, the wings of the air, and all green
things that live.

You have set the powers of the four quarters of the
earth to cross each other. You have made me cross
the good road and the road of difficulties, and where
they cross, the place is holy. Day in, day out, forever-
more, you are the life of things.

'Earth Prayer', Black Elk, Oglala Sioux mystic
(1863–1950)

Sacred Dancing: celebrating the cosmos

Do you not know that the body is the temple of the
Holy Spirit within you?

(1 Corinthians 3:16)

The form of meditation used by the Sufi dervishes is a ecstatic
dance of surrender. It is a *turn* – a dissolving of the ego and a merging into God. This dancing involves both a change in awareness
for spiritual reasons and a celebration of the holy. Dervish means
'doorway'. The poet Rainer Maria Rilke thought the whirling a
form of kneeling when he saw it. It is a dance where great discipline is needed, for the aim is to arrive at a different consciousness.
The American academic and translator of Sufi writings, Coleman
Barks explains it in this way: 'When the gravitational pull gets
ever stronger, the two [human and divine] become one turning
that is molecular and galactic and a spiritual remembering of the
presence at the centre of the universe.' (*The Essential Rumi*).

The whirling dervish becomes an empty space in this way so
that he is made into a meeting place of the human merged with
the divine. He forms a holy circle, like the great hoop found in
Native American and other spiritualities, and the wheel of eternity itself. The Muslim philosopher and mystic, Avicenna (Abu
Ali al-Hysayn Ibn Sina, 980–1037), often called 'the prince of
philosophers', described the highest degree in this Sufi sacred
dance as follows:

> He [the Dervish] looks turn by turn at God and his
> soul as in a reciprocal motion; but at the end even
> his soul disappears from his sight; he sees no longer
> anything but Holiness itself, or if he still sees his
> soul, it is inasmuch as this latter sees God. On
> arriving at this point, he has realised union.

Dance is a universal form of religious devotion. Evidence of the antiquity of dance is found in prehistoric cave paintings. It features in almost every spirituality and religious practise found in the world – ancient Egypt, classical Greece, Hindu worship, Shaker practises, Israel where Jews dance with the Torah, Christian liturgies where dancing is done before the altar, and in Africa, Australia and North America. Wherever humans are, they dance, and this dancing is a celebration of life – joy, gladness, thankfulness and pleasure in living. It opens the heart. The Sufi mystic Rumi wrote of this dancing:

> Dance when you're broken open.
>
> Dance if you've torn the bandage off.
>
> Dance in the middle of the fighting.
>
> Dance in your blood.
>
> Dance when you're perfectly free
>
> (*The Essential Rumi*)

To the person who is dancing with sacred intentions, their movements are making visible the invisible movements of the spirit. Dance can express adoration, praise, supplication and joy. It is prayer articulated not by words but by your whole body. Dance in this way becomes a spiritual practise expressing your inner feelings of homage to God.

The Bible, and the psalms in particular, treat dance as an acceptable part of religious practise. Psalm 149 tells us, 'Sing a new song to the Lord . . . praise his name with dancing.' And again in Psalm 150, 'Praise him with timbrel and dance.' The Dutch Protestant theologian, Geradus van der Leeuw wrote that

> the dance is the natural expression of the man who
> is just as conscious of his body as he is of his soul. In

the dance, the boundaries between body and soul are effaced. The body moves itself spiritually, the spirit bodily.

Despite these advocates, for many centuries Christians were not certain of the appropriateness of dancing as a form of worship. While some denominations do not object, many Christians and their churches today remain reluctant to allow dancing as part of their worship. It would appear that to them *something* might get out of control if people were to dance about, and this might make everybody uncomfortable. This says much about how most of us deny our bodies. It says even more about our attitude to our sexuality, which we too often limit by defining it only in a physical sense. This leads many people to view the body as somehow 'sinful' and to separate it from the mind and spirit as an inferior part of ourselves. This attitude, which wrongly fragments our true nature, has its roots in Platonic dualism. The Greek philosopher Plato regarded the physical body as an unclean enemy of the soul and a source of its defilement. Much of this attitude crept into Christian thinking and, whether Christian or not, we need to recognise that this view of the body is not biblical, nor does it reflect the doctrine of the world's great religions which all lay stress on the unity of the physical and the spiritual. Any spiritual tradition or religion which prescribes a life-style that deadens the body, kills the soul.

Picking and choosing from sacred texts only what seems to suit the needs of a polite assembly and rejecting that which does not, would seem less than a complete surrender of the ego to God. For many people, the history of Jesus Christ and the early years of his church tells of a religion which is not meant to be *comfortable*. When David, King of Judah and of Israel, *danced whirling round* before God wearing only a loincloth, he was criticised as making a spectacle of himself like a buffoon. King David replied he was dancing for God and that he would continue to do so (2 Samuel 6:14, 21). (It is interesting that the Old Testament tells us the way King

David danced was by *whirling*, as in the dervish Sufi practice.)

Through the instrument of our bodies, our dancing in holy celebration not only opens our hearts so the soul may dance, it is a spiritual practice that recognises God not as static symbol but as dynamic reality. Our dancing mirrors the constant movement in the universe itself. So dance your way through the Gateway of Celebration. It is prayer. It is good health. It makes you happy.

Encountering your inner child through dance

The psychologist Carl Jung believed that the image of the child represented the strongest, most inescapable urge in every human, namely the urge to realise oneself. He thought this child archetype was the symbol of psychic wholeness. All of us carry an image within of the ideal childhood we would like to have had, constructed out of our own experiences, but the inner child archetype lies at a much deeper level. It represents the creative aspects of life both within us as individuals and in our collective humanity, and has been called the 'divine child'. Perhaps it is this divine child, the pure and true self, that Jesus spoke of when he said, 'In truth I tell you, anyone who does not welcome the kingdom of God like a little child will never enter it.' (Luke 18:17). Our inner child carries our personal histories and is both the actual and the imaginary child of our past. The same child showing different faces can become a symbol for many aspects of our self – our memory, woundedness, wisdom and potential.

Psychologists such as Wilhelm Reich, E. T. Gendlin and Alice Miller seem to agree that the truth about our childhood is stored up in our bodies, and dance when it is authentic movement from within and not some planned display of movements can bring this inner child to the surface of our consciousness. Your body then becomes a non-verbal instrument for communicating subtle inner feelings, thoughts, images and symbols as they arise in you. Your body leads the truth of the self into the light of consciousness.

Your inner child speaks.

Those who have discovered the inner child within themselves seem to agree that the encounter gave them a sense of awe and wonder and a feeling of being intact at long last. As the inner child in you becomes more visible, so the various hidden aspects of yourself become more visible, and you explore your self more deeply. Contacting your inner child animates the baby, child and teenager in you, and your adult years too. You can see the story of your life in a way you never thought possible, realising the full extent of its vibrancy, pain and joy. This deeper knowledge of yourself can reveal the presence of God in your life.

You may think this sounds a lot to expect of your inner child, but it is not. The archetype is the embodiment of that immense part of yourself which dwells in the unconscious. Never underestimate the depth of your soul and the power of your spirit.

Inviting this Inner Child to appear can be done by using simple sequences of movements in a way which opens your unconscious while maintaining your conscious awareness of what is happening. Mary Whitehouse (1911–79), one of the world's most influential dance therapists, described this as 'active imagination':

> While the consciousness looms on, participating but not directing, cooperating but not choosing, the unconscious is allowed to speak whatever and however it likes. Its language appears in the form of painted or verbal images that may change rapidly – poetry, sculpture and dance. The levels they come from are not always personal levels; a universal connection with something much deeper than the personal ego is represented.

It became apparent to Mary Whitehouse that if her goal in dance therapy was to make the unconscious conscious, this process of active imagination had to be expressed in a free and non-directed manner – dance had to be done in free movements and not in some formal stylised manner. She called this 'authentic movement', and used the term 'I move' to describe the conscious controlled movements we make in formal dancing and the term 'I am moved' to describe the authentic movements of the hidden unconscious that rise to the surface and make such dancing an experience that unifies our spirit, mind and body. Dancing anchors you immediately in the present reality. Desiring is forgotten. Illusions go away. You arc living in the present moment. Your dance has made you mindful. When we are so unified we have made our dance into a celebration. Our soul rejoices in this completeness and we can offer our dancing to God with joy like King David did.

Dancing your inner child

What will you do to free your Inner Child? What authentic movements of yourself will express this hidden presence? Will it be doing a war-dance, leaping about with joy, spinning, rocking, curling up and being still, or hopping, skipping and jumping? Your body has inherent wisdom and so you do not have to *think* of your dance, but just follow the images, sensations and feelings your body offers you.

First you need to find an empty room or private place outside where you can dance. Just move as the spirit takes you.

Wear comfortable clothes that won't restrict your movements, and take your shoes off. If you do any sports, you will know about warming up before exercising. You do the same thing when you are about to start sacred dancing – even if your dance is a very modest one. Warming up will raise your consciousness of your body as well.

When you first start dancing in celebration of the holy you should remember four things: do not overtax your muscles; choose a variety of different movements; move different parts of your body; and keep a rhythm to it – after all you *are* dancing. This is a celebration.

Warming-up exercises

Body Balance

1. Stand erect, with your arms at your sides and your bare feet flat on the floor. Lift your feet so your weight is first on your heels, then on the balls of your feet; finally stand on tip-toe. Relax and stand normally. Repeat three times.

2. Place your fingertips on your shoulders. Move your right elbow forward and back; repeat with your left elbow. Do this four times. Relax.

3. Stand with your feet apart. Stretch your right arm out to the side and draw a circle in the air; repeat with your left arm. Do this four times. Relax

4. Stand with your feet together and your hands on your waist. Run on the spot for a count of ten. Relax.

What you dance must come from within you. The source of your movements is spiritual and hidden in your inner space. Let it come out. Move as the spirit moves you. Let your body describe and identify with true feelings in you. Here are some things your body might want to say: *I am delighted. I am angry. I worship. I am happy. I am sad. I withdraw from the world. I love. I am frightened. I am listening.* What feels genuine to you? Move to it. Dance to it. Be it.

If you have trouble finding movements that feel natural to you, imagining some situations may help. Here are five scenarios, some of them based on suggestions by sacred dance specialist Anne Long in her book *Praise Him in the Dance*. Use them as starting points, and then dance on from these places of imagination into your inner space. Let your dancing be a transformation that releases the original, divine child in you – the one who is deeply united in body and spirit. This sacred dancing is like a great feast

Starting points

Choose one of these to start you dancing.

1. You are crossing a stream by stepping stones, using your hands and arms to balance yourself. Are you scared?

2. You bend down to play with a cute puppy. Tickle it. Pick it up. Cuddle it. Let it chase you across the room. Are you happy?

3. You are caught by jungle vines which wrap around you. You need to free your head, arms, legs and chest. It is difficult. Bend and stretch to free yourself. Where are you going?

4. You are in a field and a storm breaks. You dart from tree to tree to find cover from the rain. Who are you?

5. You are lost in the forest. You walk in circles. Sometimes you run, then you skip, then you stand still. The circles get smaller until you are slowly turning. You stop. Where are you now?

for your body: don't be greedy and overload your senses.

After you finish your dance, ask yourself who is this child of yourself that is dancing? Is it a symbol or a memory? What does she or he want? What does she or he offer you? Meditate upon your answers.

Your dancing reunites and reconnects you to God for it is a prayer spoken by your body. As the Christian mystic, Mechthild of Magdeburg (1210–97) advised us, 'Do not disdain your body for the soul is just as safe in its body as in the Kingdom of Heaven.' So dance for joy and in celebration of who and what you are.

THE SEVENTH GATEWAY

Dreaming – The way of rediscovering unity

Our dream life is as much part of our reality as our waking life because our dreams are a dynamic world that can bring the unconscious into conscious awareness. Not only do we *live* in our dreams, but we can use this part of ourselves in spiritual ways to enlarge the whole psychic field of our sacred life. When we lift up our hidden self into the light of our ordinary life, we enter the Gateway of Dreaming. We can do this in many ways – by a shamanic vision quest which transcends ordinary realms of time and space; by being aware of the presence of guardian spirits or angels; by bringing to the surface our disowned parts and looking at what they say about our true selves; and by opening ourselves fully to our physical senses and the elements of nature.

Our dreams are visions, and our purest vision of the world should cross all boundaries, defy classification and fashion, and give us the courage to acknowledge the true intimacy of our relationship with all forms of reality. We can be changed for ever by our encounter with this world of the spirit. Many who are not yet so transformed will think us strange, confused or even mad. Others will rally to our leadership.

Everyone dreams and so everyone knows that there is a dimension outside the ordinary reality of consciousness. This other part of our being, this dreaming, has been explored and theorised about for the whole history of humanity. Dreams are the rising up of the unconscious part of ourselves, the stuff of our hopes, the forecasting of possible futures, the histories of our past, the desires and battles of our identity, the pleasures and mourning of what we cannot realise in our waking hours. When we repeatedly dream the same dream, we get a feeling that somehow, in some way, we are being told something – that there is a message waiting to be understood. It seems partially visible, not quite clear to us. Many people sense that if they could understand such a repeating dream, it might tell or warn them of some future event. Dreams have always been part of visions and visions live in the spiritual realm.

This world of dreams is part of your belonging to the universe and it is as much a part of your true reality as the end of your nose. Dreams cannot be ignored for they can haunt us, drive us to new aspirations, or bring despair. They are as connected to our past as to our future. The writer Jeanette Winterson summed it up this way in her novel *The Passion*:

> The future is foretold from the past and the future is only possible because of the past. Without past and future, the present is partial. All time is eternally present and so all time is ours. There is no sense in forgetting and every sense in dreaming. Thus the present is made rich. Thus the present is made whole.

Our dreams are a force of unity in making sense of belonging and in joining together our exterior and interior worlds which, although we may think of them as separate, are a continuous whole. Dreams mirror the endless cosmos, giving us glimpses of the unknown and bringing to us a realm entirely made of the spirit. Here is to be found the realm of experience or reality that exists outside the narrow, limited state of your normal waking consciousness. All the spirits of yourself live here, along with primordial nature and archetypes of myths that anchor us in our humanity. It is a place where truth and terror, fantasy and fable, ghosts and ancient histories abide. Dreams bring us the understanding that we possess a dimension of self hidden from ordinary consciousness. They tell us that we are not separate from the animals, plants, stones, rolling sands, far stars and endless universe of imagination. From our dreaming can come confirmation of our deep unity with other life, and this is holy.

The next time you awake from a dream, do not let it slip from your mind but hold on to its detail as much as possible. Use the elements of the dream as a meditation on yourself. Did your dream of riches speak of your hidden desire for power or change? Did the beautiful dream-lover whisper of your need for love? Did the terror of your dream reveal a fear of losing control? There are many ways to analyse our dreams, but for spiritual purposes we need to look at what they can tell us that will help us live a more whole existence.

Looking at a dream

1. What do you think the dream is about?
2. What is the major element in it? Love, fear, escape, power, anger . . . ? What does this say about your true needs?
3. Does your dream connect you in any way to other things? The sea, the earth, water, fire, animals, or mysterious beings? Are these things part of you?
4. Does your dream hold a vision of your past, the present or the future? Do you feel this vision is true of your life?

We may also encounter the dreamscape of our spiritual journey in the rare moments when our waking consciousness becomes
super-consciousness. Then we may behold visions which spring
from the desire of our soul for unity with the spirit in all life. At
that moment, if we are lucky, the Eternal Dancer who lives in our
soul awakens the shaman inside us.

Shamanic vision

Shamans, who are healers and keepers of ancient spiritual techniques, have existed in human societies since before recorded
history. They are men or women who can enter an altered state of
consciousness when they so will it. In this state they contact and
utilise a hidden spiritual reality in order to acquire power and
knowledge to help other people. They *use* the spirit world.
Shamanism as a spiritual way is becoming increasingly popular
with many people and this spiritual inheritance has never been
lost from the cultures of many native peoples. However, the
chances of you ever knowing a real shaman are slim since much of
the authenticity of shamanism exists when the shaman is an integral part of a particular society's way of life.

This does not mean that you cannot employ shamanic techniques in your spiritual life. The basics of shamanism are easy to
learn, although for effective practice much self-discipline is
required. In practising shamanism you are helping yourself to
move from a state of ordinary consciousness into your dreamscape
– a place of non-ordinary reality. You are fusing the world your five
senses knows with another world that your intuition tells you
exists. If you have not experienced the realm of non-ordinary reality, do not dismiss it. As yet no scientific research has
incontestably proven that there is only *one* reality. Recent
research in neurochemistry shows that your brain carries its own
chemistry for altering consciousness and this includes the use of

natural hallucinogens. If the theory that natural selection has provided us with nothing that is not useful for our survival is correct, your capacity for an altered state of consciousness – the dreamscape of your spiritual self – must confer on you some advantage. Mother Nature is the *wise woman* who makes each aspect of life work for the perfection of the whole.

You will probably not be surprised to learn that many athletes enter an altered state of consciousness just at the moment when they have performed their greatest sporting feat. Don't we often call their achievements *amazing, miraculous* and *unbelievable*? So why not be equally credulous when told that Tibetan holy men and Australian Aboriginal shamans can travel great distances at a super-human running rate, far beyond anything normal, when they have entered an altered state of consciousness? The mind and body are limited but the power of the spirit cannot be measured.

Drumming, rattling, singing and dancing are well-established techniques to help a shaman to enter a state of altered consciousness where they find spiritual powers of healing and vision. While in this altered state, the soul of the shaman is believed to leave his or her body and travel to the Upper World or Underworld. Each of these worlds contains a cosmic geography of non-ordinary reality that we may all glimpse from time to time in our dreams. Here is where a shaman begins the journey to find an appropriate animal, plant or other spirit power. The events and encounters they experience are as real as those found in an ordinary state of consciousness.

When a shaman sees and hears spirits, they are carried out of their ordinary reality. Mircea Eliade, one of the world's foremost authorities on comparative religion, says this state is not a trance but 'a state of inspiration', because while in this visionary state the shaman is not unconscious. In shamanic spirituality some degree of altered consciousness is necessary to enter any shamanic journey. Visualising or imagining must take place. The Australian Aborigines call it 'the strong eye'. Some type of repeating sound is often used to help a person enter this altered state. The drumbeats are in the same frequency range as the theta waves in our brains – 4 to 7 cycles per second. Research has shown that this drumming produces changes in the central nervous system, stimulating and affecting the electrical activity in sensory and motor areas of the brain. The shaking of a rattle also stimulates brain pathways and heightens the total sonic effect. Singing or repetitive chanting can achieve similar effects.

The angels of grace: guardianship and protection

Shamanic knowledge is basically consistent around the world irrespective of variation among primitive peoples as to their social systems, art, economies and other aspects of culture and social organisation. The starting point of this knowledge is the guardian spirit. Without one you cannot be a shaman. The guardian spirit is a base power source for coping with the elements of the spirit world. In shamanism this guardian spirit is often a powerful animal who in spirit form protects the shaman and becomes his or her alter ego or identity. To a shaman animals have powerful spirits and can help people in specific ways. The relationship between the shaman and the animal spirit is one of mutual benefit where the shaman offers respect and loyalty and the animal spirit offers guidance and assistance. Guardianship and protection are one of the principle roles of the animal spirit. It is believed that each animal spirit has particular talents. For example, the bull has strength, the fox cunning, and the mouse stealth. We reflect these beliefs in our everyday language – we may speak of a person being as strong as a bull or sly as a fox or quiet as a mouse. This kind of endowment of animals with spiritual powers is used extensively in advertising – among the most famous being the tiger in your petrol tank. Most children and many adults dream of animals with magical powers, and certainly children easily and quickly give animal toys a life of their own – just think of the newspaper cartoon character Hobbs. Most animal spirits are wild ones, and the shaman finds them through allowing them to enter into his or her consciousness during dancing or chanting or, more usually, through a vision. Wherever we turn in art, folklore, literature, religion, mythology and sacred texts we find these guardian spirits, who also often take the form of winged beings or angels.

In the Bible, Abraham's hand is stayed from sacrificing his son by an angel of God. Another angel informs Mary that she will give birth to the Christ. Then there is the most famous fallen angel Lucifer, about whom the poet Milton wrote in *Paradise Lost*. These guardian spirits act as intermediaries between humans and the Divine in Judaism, Christianity, Hinduism, Buddhism, and Islam. According to tradition, Mohammed the Prophet was asleep one night when three angels came to him, cut open his chest and took out his heart. They washed his heart in the water of the sacred well of ZamZam in Mecca and cleansed from him all doubt, idolatry, paganism and error. Then they filled up the cavity in his chest with Wisdom, replaced his heart and sewed up his chest. On the next night as he lay in perfect stillness between waking and sleeping, the Angel Gabriel appeared to him and he was transported into mystical union with the Eternal. This is how the story is often told:

> Suddenly Gabriel the Archangel descended in his own form. Of such beauty, of such sacred glory, of such majesty, that all my dwelling was illuminated. He is of a whiteness brighter than snow, his face is gloriously beautiful, the waves of his hair fall in long tresses, his brow is encircled as with a diadem of light on which is written, 'There is no god but God'. He has six hundred wings set with 70,000 grains of red chrysolite. When he approached me, he took me in his arms, kissed me between the eyes and said, 'O sleeper, how long wilt thou sleep? Arise! Tenderly will I guide thee. Fear not, for I am Gabriel thy brother.'

> (*Angels*, Peter Lamborn Wilson, Thames and Hudson, London, 1980)

The great shaman and visionary, Black Elk, was a major force in the revival of Native American spirituality in this century. This is how he described the angelic encounter that gave him a healing mission not just to his own people at a time when they needed it, but for all humanity:

> I looked up at the clouds, and two men were coming down, head first like arrows slanting down; and as they came, they sang a sacred song and the thunder was like drumming. I will sing it for you. The song and drumming were like this: 'Behold, the sacred voice is calling you! All over the sky a sacred voice is calling!'

In our Western culture, Christianity, with its emphasis on a single and supreme manifestation of the divine in human form, may lead us to miss this sense of spiritual guardianship and the angelic possibilities of love. Modern people feel ill at ease before many manifestations of the sacred, finding it difficult to accept, for example, that for some people the sacred may be manifested in stones or trees. What should never be forgotten is that the veneration is not for the stone or tree itself, but because they show something which is no longer understood as mineral or vegetable matter but as sacred – the *wholly other* of Creation. In the same way, angels and other messengers may appear in our lives. They too represent the Creation of God.

Your sacred role

We are all shamans in the sense that we do not live separated from the spiritual nor from altered states of consciousness. We too can possess healing powers that cannot be explained by physical or mental properties. We too exist in a one-to-one relationship with the Eternal in all its many forms – the stone, the tree, the angel, the animal spirits. This means you have a sacred role, for you are the high priestess of yourself. As light has dark, the sun the moon, and stars the sky, so you too are both male and female in the spirit. Your body, empowered by your mind, is your temple; your soul is the altar. Here is the place of mystical union where if you are fortunate you may glimpse the eternal. There is nothing in this life of which you are not a part. Unseen depths exist in everything that surrounds you. When you hear the voice of the wolf or the wind, know that they are within you. By practising the sacred, you honour your spiritual self and make visible within you that which cannot be seen with the eye.

Do not think for one moment that spiritual vision or revelations belong to just religious people or to specially gifted ones. While it is true that such revelations are divine gifts, we do not have to earn one before we get it. Holy visions or revelations often come to ordinary people and, although they may never talk about them, such events change their life because they have gained a new insight into its meaning. This may have already happened to you – or it may happen the next time you step through the Gateway of Dreaming into the garden of your soul.

From time to time in the history of the world there have been visions that transformed the spiritual life not just of the people who had them, but of generations of people. Such visions have often given evidence of the spiritual world through miracles and other phenomena. They should encourage us all to believe we are destined to live a sacred life, and to enter the Gateway of Dreaming in search of our own visions.

One such vision was that of Marie Bernarde Soubirous (1844–79), a fourteen-year-old peasant girl known today as St Bernadette of Lourdes. She received no less than eighteen visions of Mary, the mother of Jesus, at the Massabielle Rock in Lourdes, over a period of months. During this time, a spring appeared in the grotto at the rock, the waters of which are believed to be miraculous. Almost immediately after her visions, people started visiting the grotto to seek cures for their illnesses and fulfilment of their prayers. The Roman Catholic Church, to which Marie-Bernarde belonged, is medically and ethically rigorous in deciding if any claim of a cure is authentic. There have been a small but impressive number of cases declared miracles over the years, the most recent in 1998.

All the world's great spiritualities have places like Lourdes that are holy and that can help us access the hidden realities of the self – Mecca, Fatima, Mount Sinai, the mountain of the Lakota. Yet the list of such places is short when compared to the number of revelations that have taken place inside the hearts and souls of countless women and men. To enter the Gateway of Dreaming is to confirm that you are on a similar journey to discover this sacred aspect of yourself.

Dark spirits: light on darkness

As there is the visible, so there is the invisible. As there is light, so there is the darkness. Our guilty feelings are inner burdens, hiding in the dark corners of ourselves. The darkness, sometimes called *the passage of purgation*, cannot be avoided in our spiritual journey.

Are there parts of yourself that you have disowned? The dark forces of your personality that you unconsciously hide? Stop resisting disclosure. Bring them to the surface and know them for what they are. Become emotionally whole. No one is nice all the time, so admit you feel awful about something you did or said. Better yet, tell someone how you feel. You will have shone light on your darkness.

In this realm of the spiritual there are many opposites. As good can exist, so can evil. Michael Harner, the American scholar who has helped pioneer the modern shamanic renaissance, records that while he was visiting the Conibo Indians of the Amazon he entered a shamanic state in which he saw a reptile with water gushing out of its mouth and feared for his life. When he later described this to some Christian missionaries, they were not surprised but read him the following line from the Bible: 'And the serpent cast out of his mouth water as a flood . . .' As I discussed earlier in this book, throughout the mythology of the world serpents are often synonymous with Satan, the Devil, and Universal Darkness. The nature of evil is disharmony which rightly inspires fear. It is a denial of good and a forgetting of compassion that still casts terrible shadows on our world. In searching for that which is sacred and holy, do not call upon dark spirits nor dismiss their existence, but take as your guide this wisdom from the Qur'an: 'Be steadfast in prayer, enjoin justice and forbid evil'.

The vision quest

Traditionally a vision quest is undertaken by someone who is seeking a guardian spirit. They seek in the spiritual realm those powers that the mind and body do not offer. The vision quest was called 'Lamenting for a Dream' by the Lakota Sioux of the Plains People of America. Such a spiritual journey is sacred and important. It is a pilgrimage in your interior realm to find personal spiritual power and to use it for inner guidance to clarify things in your ordinary life, including healing and the exercise of spiritual virtues such as patience and love. Vision quests take many forms around the world and may be done in special places such as a Native American sweat lodge. There are, however, traditionally some common elements in a vision quest and these have been incorporated into the following exercises.

Preparation and initiation for a vision quest is not undertaken lightly. If you decide to make a contemporary vision quest based on the shamanic tradition you should also take it very seriously.

Fasting is traditional before making a vision quest, so if you can fast all the better (see the section on fasting in the Gateway of Prayer). If you cannot fast, then try to eat very lightly – stick to vegetables and don't consume alcohol, meat or stimulants like tea and

172 THE SEVENTH GATEWAY

coffee. You will also need to spend some time gathering what you need to make the quest, such as drums or rattles, and practising some of the skills required for a vision quest itself such as drumming, rattling, chanting, becoming more aware of your senses, and opening your heart to the spiritual in the natural elements around you.

You can buy a drum suitable for shaman work, including those that resemble traditional Native American shamanic drums. The best drum to use is a small one with a single head that is easy to hold in one hand – about 40–44 cm (16–17 in) in diameter. Play it by hitting it with the palm of one or both hands in a single, repetitive beat. You can, of course, construct your own drum and there are craft books about making such instruments. You can also buy drumming tapes to use: these are as good as beating a real drum because it is the sound that is important.

You can buy a rattle easily enough or you can make one yourself without too trouble. Take a clean small glass jar, drop in a dozen or so dried beans, screw on the lid, and you have got yourself a rattle. Shake it in a repetitive manner to make a beat.

Shamans often have power songs that they chant on their shamanic journey to the spirit world. These songs tend to be highly repetitive, simple and monotonous. They usually keep increasing in tempo without any change in the words or sound formations. They appear to have a similar effect to drumming on the central nervous system, although there has been little research on this. The use of chanting is widespread among all religions and spiritual practices, including Christianity. Monks and nuns have told me that they often find themselves in a trance-like state when the chanting of the psalms in their choir goes on too long.

You can buy recordings of chants, including those used by native peoples. The hymns originated and used at Taizé, the ecumenical Christian centre in France, are so repetitive that some people find them mesmerising. You can also purchase special shamanic tapes that combine chanting, drumming and rattling.

Shamans often find songs in their dreams. Robert L. Oswalt

in his *Kashaya Texts*, tells us of a Pomo Indian shaman, Essie Parrish, who told this story about dreaming her power song:

> I'm going to tell you another story about when I was young – about how I first sang when I was a child. I was eleven years old at that time. I didn't acquire that song in any ordinary way – I dreamed it. One time, as I lay asleep, a dream came to me – I heard singing up in the sky. Because I was little, because I didn't realise what it was, I didn't pay attention to it – I just listened when that man was singing up above. Still he made it known to me – it was as if it entered deep into my chest, as if the song itself were singing in my voice box. Then it seems as if I could see the man, as if I could just make him out. After I awoke from sleep, that song was singing inside me all day long. Even though I didn't want to sing, still the song was singing in my voice box. Then I myself tried, tried to sing, and amazingly the song turned out beautiful. I have remembered it ever since.

So if you find yourself dreaming a song, recall it in your waking reality, use it to enter your shaman space.

Open your heart to nature's spirits

We protect ourselves from the blessing of rain. We keep the wind from embracing our bodies. We mask our eyes against sunlight. We treat ourselves like fragile creatures, resisting the sensations of truly living in the natural elements of earth. Even our nights are made light by lamps. This is a great pity for it separates us from a sense of belonging to the rise and fall of our sun, the phases of the moon, and the world of night itself. All elements have their source in the spirit world. Shamans speak with the wind, the air, the earth, the clouds, the sun and the moon.

Dress yourself in robes of wind. When a strong wind blows, go out and welcome it. Stretch out your arms, close your eyes. Ride the wind through forests, through city streets and fields of grass. You are travelling with a spirit of imagination. You are embracing nature's spirit. You are Sister Wind

Go out for a walk in veils of moonlight. When the moon is full go for a walk in safe countryside, away from urban lighting. Sit on the ground. Watch Mother Moon as her gentle light moves through clouds; see the stars in her halo. Imagine the land of her invisible side. Think of the stream of humanity that has looked upon her. If you were to say something to Mother Moon what would it be? Can you imagine a life without her?

Awareness Exercises
Singing from your inner voice
Open your mouth wide and sing out all the words that come into your head. Never mind what you are saying: the sense is in the sounds. Use your voice to let out your inner feelings. As you sing, chant or even sigh, you release yourself into the freedom of the spirit.

A day with your five senses
Your senses are gifts of magic. Make today a time for discovering the marvels of your five senses. Really taste what you eat. Massage and feel your hands and feet. Listen to beautiful music. Smell a flower. Count the colours of sunset. The more conscious you are of these gifts the easier it will be for you to enter other realms of consciousness, as you will do on your vision quest.

Choosing a time, place and a question

When you have chosen and practised your instruments and chanting and done the above exercises to increase your inner awareness and stillness, you must consider the time and place for your vision quest and choose the question that you will take with you to be answered in the realm of the spirit.

Decide how long your inner journey will be. A short time is just as good as a long one and the journey should take place when you are most free of commitments that may be pressing on your mind. An important date like your birthday or an anniversary of some happy event are also good choices. As to place, it must be quiet, free of people and interruptions, and preferably out in the open. You could choose a quiet spot along your favourite woodland walk or even a secret corner of your garden. If you can go to a place that holds strong feelings for you or has historic spiritual connections, these can help you. Take nothing with you which could distract you from making your inner journey – no radios or mobile phones.

Reflect on why you are making a vision quest. Are you about to make an important choice in your life, looking for an answer to a specific problem, or doing it for the sake of enriching your spiritual experience? Perhaps you wish to meet your guardian spirit and to call forth this protection to help you in your life? In any case, you are going on a journey of the spirit and when you pass through the Gateway of Dreaming into the garden of your soul, you will want to make best use of your time there. Praying about your vision quest before you begin can be helpful.

As soon as possible after your quest, write down your vision and what you felt was the meaning of it. The message may be clear and direct – go ahead with buying that house or applying for that new job, or a realisation that it is time for a change of lifestyle. In many cases the message will be wrapped up as if in the form of a dream. Then you have to look at it symbolically and discover what sense it makes in terms of your life – its meaning will probably become clear as time passes, so don't try analysing it too much.

Often people find that although they may not exactly understand the message they found in their vision quest, they get a new slant on a situation or on themselves. Do not worry if you did not have a vision or get any messages, because insights do not always happen right away. Perhaps days will pass or even months and years until they do, because where you have gone, as in all dreams, is a timeless place. As with all aspects of living a sacred life, the more you practise making a shamanic journey, the better you will get at it. So make a vision quest whenever you feel you need one. The Gateway of Dreaming, like all the gateways to open the heart, is always there for you.

The vision quest journey

When you feel ready, try this vision quest, which is based on shamanic traditions.

1. Having found a quiet, private place where you are sure you will not be disturbed, lie down on the ground. Hold your rattle in one hand or have your drum or tape-recorder controls within easy reach.

2. Take ten minutes or so to become very calm. Close your eyes and breathe gently until your mind and body are relaxed. Let yourself dwell in your inner space. Be at rest and at ease with yourself. Let all worries and desires fade away. Be filled with stillness.

3. Begin to gently sound your rattle, holding it close to your ear, or start your chant, drumming or tape. Keep the sound going continuously from now until the end of this quest when you return to ordinary reality. Gradually increase the tempo if you are rattling, drumming or chanting. Let the sounds echo inside you. Let yourself surrender *into* the sound. Let it fill you up like water poured into a glass. Swim in it, drink it, become the sound itself. You are going through the Gateway of Dreaming.

4. Let all inner sounds and images of ordinary life pass from you. Begin to feel detached from ordinary things. Keep the sound going.

5. Now let your imagination soar. Give it free rein to go

Our dreaming brings forth many aspects of the spiritual realm, some familiar and many beyond all we have previously known or understood. In the sacred all things are possible, and the unconscious may be transformed into the living moment of the present. The Gateway of Dreaming is there every day in our sleep, our imagination and the life of our souls. It has these words inscribed above it: 'For God everything is possible.'

---

anywhere. See with your inner eye the dreamscape of your inner self. If there is a persistent sense or vision of the presence of a guardian spirit or power animal, whether it is like a real one or not, let it stay with you. Greet it and let the image become strong and vivid. Have no fear, for God is always with you, as Psalm 90 tells us: 'Upon you no evil shall fall, no plague approach where you dwell, for you has he commanded his angels to keep you in all your ways.'

6. Ask your guardian spirit or power animal for insight into your life – ask them the question you prepared earlier. Listen carefully.

7. Thank your guardian spirit or power animal and let it go from your inner vision.

8. Keeping your eyes closed, stop rattling/drumming/ chanting/turn off the tape and return yourself to ordinary reality. Ground yourself by becoming aware of your face and hair, and by feeling the earth or floor beneath you. Breathe in the smells of the world around you.

9. Meditate on how you feel. Let any thoughts linger in your mind so you can consider them. If you are moved to pray, do so.

10. When you have come to the end of the time you allotted, give thanks for the place you are in, and when you get up leave no evidence that you have been there.

THE EIGHTH GATEWAY

Affirmation – The way of taking stock

Belief consists in accepting the
affirmations of the soul; Unbelief in
denying them.

Uses of Great Men: Montaigne, Ralph Waldo Emerson
(1803–82)

Our lives are always busy with making personal life choices. Some bring us happiness and others regret, but the choices we make are up to us. That is the paradox of our free will which is both a gift and a burden. It is also the paradox of the Gateway of Affirmation, for this ancient way of the spirit is opened by our hopes and dreams, our gratitude for all the good in our lives, and our thankfulness for the existence of life itself. The paradox is that it is also opened by facing up to the reality of the sad and bad in our lives, all our downs and disappointments, and the times when we lose sight of our direction and dreams for the future. These challenges also open the gateway because in working our way through them we can choose to affirm ourselves and our dreams and reclaim a belief in the worth of our true selves. In this way we know God is still with us and, affirming this awareness, we can enter once again into the garden of the soul. As life is choices, so is the Gateway of Affirmation. It is there for us not just to be thankful but to find in our lives the things to be thankful for. It is a way of taking stock so we can affirm what we need and want and bring it into our lives now and not at some future time. When we affirm our real feelings we are becoming true to ourselves and this brings God close right away.

There are many ways to respond to situations and these prompt the choices we make. We need to acquire an extraordinary consciousness of what is actually going on inside us to make our responses positive and an affirmation of our lives. We can begin the way through the gateway by considering a few of these situations and how they affect our spiritual well-being. We can learn to increase our awareness of the blessings in our lives – the affirmation of the positive things which make us feel good and of which there is usually an abundance. The first thing we need to do is to keep a spiritual vision right up front in our consciousness so that it influences our choices in a positive and godly way and helps to affirm our life.

Keeping the spiritual vision alive

Perceptions do form us. We observe the particular and from these many moments of life we build a comprehensive picture of what we believe to be reality. In this way we develop a background for our consciousness of what the world is like. This background is like a big screen on which the events in our life are projected. These are seen by us as a vision of reality. So the images we put into our minds do count and this naturally includes religious and spiritual images.

Until very recently the images we saw were slow-moving and familiar because our lives were equally slow-moving. Nothing was truly instant. We had time to correct mistakes, remake our vision, gain confidence and double-check that our big screen vision was still right for us before we moved onward. All that is changed. We still know the difference between the real and the artificial, but the background screen of our perceptions is now filled with a multitude of artificial realities, most of which are dark and cast no light upon our way through life. It becomes harder to discern what is true and what is mere imagination or conjecture. Our vision of reality becomes unstable and ever-changing. A coherent vision of the world becomes impossible and the big screen against which we judge things is as fragmented as our lives. We need enormous courage to hold steady a vision of things which are eternal, infinite and beyond human creation such as the value and benefits of a spiritual life and the reality of the immanent creative force of God.

Instead our vision becomes one that depends upon our senses – the most limited part of ourselves and the most likely to mislead us. Our definition of our self becomes based on human imaginings rather than on holy inspiration. In essence we define ourselves even at the spiritual level as mere consumers. We need a background screen that reflects spiritual wisdom. Our human heritage of these truths is a treasure-house open to everyone. All the excess of information and other things which fragment us need be of no concern. Hearts which are open to God's spirit regardless of the rushing noises and images of a busy world encourage Wisdom. She raises up her hand to stop time so we may understand, like St Augustine did, that time has no measure for the human spirit. Wisdom has no sense of time at all. She blinks and Rome falls. She smiles and religions vanish. She brings us the vision of the possibility of immortality and makes this yearning a passage to the sacred. This keeps before us a grand and mysterious invitation which leads us to ground all things in spiritual understanding. This is the big screen against which we measure true reality.

Reviewing the state of your spiritual life

Having visualised a big screen in your mind, project against it how your relationship with the holy is going at the moment. Do you feel fragmented? Are you are at peace deep inside your inner space or is it dark there? Does love embrace you or do you sense a need for more loving? Does the truth about yourself displease you or can you find happy acceptance in your true self? As you look around at the world does nature seem a gift to make you glad? Do you feel God is near or would your spirit like to spend more time in the stillness of the soul? When you relax, sit back and take a break, does a sense of happiness fill you up?

Find a notebook and list your answers to the above questions. Write down on one side of the pages all the positive things and on the other side all the negative things. Keep this notebook at hand to use as you read the following.

Hopes and dreams

To be without hopes and dreams for the future is to be in a place of loss. When we give up hoping and dreaming we hit rock bottom. We then need our spirit to lift us up by whispering to our heart: 'Control over your life is an illusion.' This is a good thing to accept and gets you out of the pits, because then you can ask for advice and help from your family, friends, and God. They are bound to encourage you because they love you. This gets your hopes and dreams up and running again. Our human nature is not naturally pessimistic: we like to hope in a brighter tomorrow. You may be poor today, but who knows who wins tomorrow. You lost the job, but somewhere surely there will be another. He left you – well, there are lots of fish in the sea. And so the list of our possibilities is always longer than our current disappointments. Our dreams bring lots of possibilities and these hopes push us forward in ordinary life and make our spirit glad, giving us reason to be thankful. Our dreams are not limited by the possible, and that makes them very exciting. Dreams stretch our current life towards new horizons and bring us the material with which to affirm what we need and want and to make it happen now. Then we swim again to the surface of our sea of disappointments and failures and find the life raft of hope. The American poet Emily Dickinson wrote that 'hope is the thing with feathers that perches in the soul and sings the tune without words and never stops at all.' To discover that which binds the world together in peace rather than to emphasise what separates us from others, is to let such hope flourish. Then we can see that all things, events and people in our lives are part of us in this peace and that is good, for God will not tolerate that you should be disappointed in his Creation. This is the nature of true hope, because it can help you transcend ordinary life and keep your vision of the holy steady. When you take stock of events and people in this way, you affirm life, and that is an act of love. You pass easily through the Gateway of Affirmation.

Open your notebook and list your hopes and dreams. Then imagine putting them one by one up on the big screen and shine the light of spiritual values on them. Which ones clearly tell of your true feelings? Which ones express the needs of your heart? Which ones would bring you the greatest joy? Which ones give you the greatest hope in your future? The hopes and dreams that pass this test are the ones to affirm. Pick one of them to act on now. First ask it to become a blessing in your life, then take it into your ordinary life by making it happen. For example, if you really want that promotion, go as soon as possible to your boss and talk about it. If the time has come for you to have a child or to let a grown-up one leave the nest, then act on your inner voice and trust your intuition – taking care to treat anyone else involved with equal respect. If you need to be quiet, book a retreat and find sanctuary and silence as soon as possible. Whatever your hopes and dreams, affirm them now.

Optimum health

Counting the blessings we already possess as well as making them happen in the future is also an act of affirmation. Doing this is a powerful way to say 'Yes!' to life. It wakes up the soul, snaps the mind to attention and quickens healthy responses in the body. It is simply *good* for you.

However, this saying 'Yes!' to life comes hard for people who are plagued by depression. So many of the stresses and strains of life can bring about a depressed state that just doesn't seem to lift. Professional health help needs to be sought when such depression dominates and begins to distort and destroy our life, but there is often scope for us to help ourselves because the answers are usually inside us. The Gateway of Affirmation can provide a way through one of the distressing features of depression which is when a person cannot break the cycle of their negative thoughts. The vicious circle of negativity goes on and on. One depressing thought follows another. This does not just mean that a depressed person's attitude is negative. It goes deeper than that, for such thinking results in biochemical changes in the body which alter its physical state, resulting, for instance, in chronic anxiety, constant irritation or an inability to sleep. Any treatment for depression is designed to interrupt this pattern of negativity.

If you suffer from depression, it is common to have feelings of emptiness. This feeling of emptiness becomes a vast void inside you, a dark hole of true loneliness. A sense of hopelessness takes over and negative thoughts go round and round inside your head – 'No one cares.' 'Life has no meaning.' 'Nothing will ever work for me.' 'Why me?' Many of us also have these negative thoughts from time to time even though we may not be suffering from what we would call depression. In such moments we feel despair at our human condition. The void opens inside us and there is a empty place which has not been filled. Something is missing: the holy vision that beyond the events of our ordinary life and consciousness lies a grander and more rewarding view of human life. Such a vision when you renew it can lift you from disappointment in your ordinary and often tedious daily life to a grander inspiration of what life is really about. This puts your life in a positive perspective.

All consciousness of our suffering arises from the emptiness deep inside that happens when we lose this vision. This empty place can only be filled by recognising this bigger picture and trying to live life as a spiritual being – not an earthbound creature who is born, feeds and dies, but like a creature who has been given free will and is burning with the holy flame of yearning for God. A person who holds dear the jewel of the heart, our dream of immortality.

If you are to realise this great destiny, you must turn away from a self-awareness that depends upon external worldly values that do not affirm your life and which will always sooner or later bring disappointment and disquiet. Instead, turn towards those values which transform our narrow and limited view of life and make us people of vision whose lives are based on a more universal view of our humanity – that life does have meaning and most people do care.

The secret is that the space that appears empty inside me when I feel so low is not really empty, because it is the place where my soul lives. When we feel this state of emptiness, the garden of the soul is hidden in darkness of our own making. Even the eyes of my heart cannot then see a way into this dwelling place of God. It is indeed the dark night of my soul for I have forgotten that my life is holy, that its purpose is to love, that I belong to God and not to the passing concerns of daily life. We need to keep the lights on in our inner space so that in illuminating the sacred in us, we bring the light of our true self into the world around us. We need to rejoice in life so that emptiness and meaninglessness will be replaced by the spirit of hope which is always holy in nature because it affirms life.

Take out your notebook again and write down these three words: money, forgiveness, success. These will be pivot points on which to act in a way which makes you feel good, which helps affirm your life and keeps the bigger vision up front.

Thinking differently about money

Stop thinking about how much you need more money or, if you are wealthy, stop thinking about what to do with it all. Instead, take some money – at least a little more than you feel you can really afford. Give this money away today. Do not send it in an envelope to some charity and do not make a note to deduct it from your income tax. This is going to be a gift from your heart and you are going to give it away completely and freely. Keep this money with you and when you next see someone begging or someone who you know needs a little extra cash, give your money to them. When they thank you, do not turn away from their thanks but receive it into your heart. In this way you acknowledge your goodness and God sees nothing wrong in that for he *wants* you to be perfect. This act of compassion in which you give away what you yourself may need is a sharing that unites you to others. You are not alone in this world and what you have is *always* more than someone else somewhere. So you have cause to be thankful.

Thinking differently about forgiveness

Here is something harder for most people to give away than their money, because it usually involves their pride – and pride is a great hindrance to affirmation because it is the result of illusions about yourself. Pride affirms nothing that is true. Is there someone in your life whom you could forgive? Perhaps a colleague at work, a member of your family or a partner who has hurt you? Affirm the positive side of life today by going to that person and forgiving them. Clear the air so that the bigger vision of life remains in clear sight.

Thinking differently about success

There is not a person in the whole world who should call themselves unsuccessful because our true success lies in discovering and knowing our true selves, which leads us to know God. Here is the kind of success that raises us above the world's ideas of fame, fortune, respectability and worthiness and puts us squarely into the eternal. No matter who you are, you would be overjoyed with that kind of success because it affirms your true nature and destiny, and helps you to get there by recognising the success you already hold. Think about your successes not in grand terms but modest ones. Perhaps you are good at gardening or knitting or cooking? Perhaps your success is in knowing how to listen or please people? Perhaps it is your ability to be patient or cheerful? Bring your own successes into your thinking, see their worth, and know they tell you about positive and true things about yourself. This illumination lights your way through the Gateway of Affirmation.

Making change a blessing

Change is the very essence of life. To stop changing is to be dead, for all life is in a constant state of flux – adaptation and alteration are the gears that let us go forward. We are not the same from microsecond to microsecond. The problem with change arises when we either use it to avoid facing up to a reality about ourselves or when we fight it and will not believe in the potential of change for good in our lives.

Children have a natural love of change for novelty attracts them and this is very much part of growing up. But some people become addicted to change. They are always changing houses, jobs, locations, even partners. The external challenges and stimulation that these changes bring allow them to avoid confronting their inner reality. When problems come up, they can use change as a ticket to new people and new surroundings. Novelty is their drug of choice and they become good at running away from themselves. Unfortunately, they carry all their emotional baggage with them. This is a corruption of the true nature of change and does nothing to help you live the sacred.

While children welcome change as natural and fun, as we grow older most of us settle down and enjoy the certainty of our habits. They have a familiarity we treasure. We can quickly form these habits into the details that make up our life. How we do this or that. When we go here or there. How we tackle certain situations. Which hymns we sing in church. What we do every Saturday morning. We become creatures of habit that want our lives to be just so right down to the last moment in the day when we lay our heads on a pillow that is just so. How easily this seduces us into believing that we have control over change. We lull ourselves into thinking we have tamed this formidable force of life.

Now we all love the comforts of our habits, but such a state of living ignores the nature of the universe. It causes illusions and desires to flourish and the ego loves this state of affairs because it stops your pilgrimage of spiritual discovery. When you fight change you are usually not affirming your own life because you are not affirming the nature of the universe itself. Accepting change is that important.

How do you feel about change?

Here are some questions to help you focus on change. Meditate on your responses to them and ask yourself how long you think you would feel that way.

1. Would you change if you were fired from your job tomorrow? How? How long would this change in you last?

2. What if the doctor told you that you had an incurable disease? What would you do?

3. Do you really think you would be happier living in a sunny climate like Florida, southern Spain or Greece? Why? How long would this change in you last?

We always think we can predict how long we will feel upset or changed by a new situation, but the fact is we are notoriously bad at making predictions about how we would feel if something really dramatic happened in our lives. Studies have shown that even severe events like the death of a loved one have a negative impact on a person's life for only about three months. This is in spite of that fact that the great majority of people in such a situation predict it would take them years to recover. Naturally there are exceptions to this, but it has been generally found that we forget our considerable capacity for making the best of a bad situation. How we actually deal with life changes is to recall our past successes, talk up our triumphs and excuse our failures and mistakes. From Freud onwards psychologists have confirmed how artful we humans are at such coping. We ignore, augment, transform and rearrange events to diminish unhappy and sad feelings and to promote a more positive present moment for ourselves.

Yet we forget that the mind works this way and that even bad changes can be naturally coped with or even discounted. We usually know what makes us feel good or bad but get it wrong when we predict how strongly and how long we might feel that way and how long the effects will last. It would appear that we have a built-in ability to cope with change, so why fear it so much? The next time unexpected changes happen in your life which you fear might be negative, have more confidence in the nature of God and the universe. Like Creation itself you are always evolving and changing and becoming.

Acknowledge and affirm the changes in your life – the little ones and the big ones. Ride with them into your future, knowing that change is almost the very definition of life. In affirming this you are eternally young, singing out from your heart like the visionary Angelae de Fulginio: 'This whole world is full of God!' You recognise with a deep intuition the true reality of change and affirm it. You will be impatient with the petty habits of the ego, knowing that within you is an innate capacity to cope. Since God is love, you will not be tested beyond your strength.

Staying connected to the sacred

When we have entered the Gateway of Affirmation we want right away to confirm the importance of the sacred in our lives by staying with this sense of the holy. But how are we to remain all the time with God when we are so busy with our families, homes, work and relationships? This is not centuries ago when the pace of life was slower. We are not monks or nuns or people who may think of themselves as being especially religious. The majority of us are modern people living in the media age, the age of instant global communications and an overabundance of information. The world is no longer a big place – it is a small planet crowded with other people where anyone can fly anywhere in a few hours. To keep in touch with the sacred, we must make a habit of our awareness of God's presence by bringing him into all aspects of our ordinary life.

Here are some ways that will help you. If you have tried them before and they are not yet a habit, then start again. I don't think many of us could do all of them all at once but I think the way to get started is to do one of them for a week until you get the hang of it, then add another way, and so on until after a while you are in the habit of practising all of them. This will help you enter the Gateway of Affirmation because each habit is a confirmation of your gladness in yourself and God.

1. Speak to God with love at all times without limiting or hiding anything in your conversation. This is especially important when you are tempted, sorrowful, feeling separated from God, or when you have been unfaithful to him, falling into abuse of your body and mind and neglecting your spirit. Your relationship with God should be a no-holds-barred one. There are no secrets, so don't kid yourself about your motives or how you really feel.

2. Reveal your heart to God as you go through your day. Try to talk to God in easy little ways while you do your work and go about the ordinary business of your life. Let the words you use arise naturally from your heart.

3. Before you act, offer your efforts to God. Whatever actions you take, do them gently, calmly and with love. Use care and try not to be impetuous – you will feel better and so will everyone around you. This brings you nearer to God and the nearer you get, the closer God gets to you.

4. Stop now and then to thank God and recall your blessings. Frequent gratitude renews hope. It is a common mistake of people who want a spiritual life to forget to put aside the routines of daily life from time to time in order to thank God and rest in his holy peace for a few minutes. So instead of a coffee break, try a thank-God break. It is the pause that refreshes the spirit!

5. Believe that God is aware of everything that happens to you. We belong to the Holy and should give it our thoughts, words and actions so that our vision of life is less one of an earthbound creature and more one of a heaven-sent angel. Sometimes just keeping going is a great act of faith, a saying *yes* to the next moment and the next and the next. The more you keep your eyes on the grand and beautiful, the easier it is to deal with the petty and difficult. If you look at your feet, you may miss the rainbow.

6. Confess to God that you need help when you find the struggle really overwhelming. When my weaknesses have tripped me up – and they do a lot of the time – and I feel I am making a real mess of my life, it is then I need an injection of God's grace. We get this healing medicine that helps us to cope by remembering that God loves us. If you are good enough for God, then why be so worried about your success or failure in worldly affairs? In such moments of concern you have let your ego rule and have ceased to be *with* God. We forget that we are not

struggling alone. Help is as close as the air we breathe. We forget God again and again and again. Yet there is virtue even in this failure, for in the struggle to live a sacred life we repeatedly rediscover all the virtues and values that bring God close. This ebb and flow in the fortunes of our spiritual life is a pilgrimage of the highest order.

Affirming your life right now

Learning to affirm your life is a tonic for your self-esteem. Here is a Native American affirmation of thanksgiving that will help you get started.

> When you arise in the morning,
>
> Give thanks for the morning light.
>
> Give thanks for your life and strength.
>
> Give thanks for your food
>
> And give thanks for the joy of living.

Affirmation guidelines

1. When you affirm your life you should confirm what is happening in the here and now of your life. Do not affirm what you *think* may happen in the future but stay in the present. Be mindful of reality. For example, don't say, 'I'll get that promotion next month.' Instead look at how your life is today in a positive way: 'I have a good job now.' Don't say, 'I'll get a bigger house soon' but 'Where I live is fine.' In other words, make where you are and what is happening to you now into affirmations. No matter who you are or how much or how little you have, this is the way to have some dignity about yourself. How you are *now* is real.

2. Affirm only what is good and don't hide little secret wishes in your affirmation. Say, for example, 'Our relationship is loving' instead of, 'Our relationship is getting better'. Affirm what is positive in the moment.

3. Affirmations stick better in your head when you write them down. Always use the first person when writing and speaking any affirmation. When you write it, make it absolutely personal by using your full name. For example, 'I, Emma Hopkins, am a healthy and loving person.' Awareness of your true self is your goal. Open your notebook and look again at the positive things you wrote down when you reviewed the state of your spiritual life. Do you still feel the same way? If so, fine, but otherwise make a new list that is closer to how you now feel and make it very personal, as I suggested. Stick the list on the wall in your bedroom or bathroom or on the fridge. Read it at least once a day. When you feel low, use it to remind yourself how worthy you are and what is important in your life.

4. Practise affirming only one thing on your list at a time. Don't crowd your mind with a lot of them – give each one real time to work. Think of your affirmations as seeds. You are planting them one by one in the garden of your soul. There they grow together and give you a positive view of your life. Say your affirmation aloud, sending it out to yourself and to God. Use your affirmation as the beginning of a prayer or before you set out for work or face an important moment in your life. Constantly reminding yourself of spiritual things keeps your spirit alive and brings your life balance and oneness.

Finding your blessings

Our lives can often seem boring and unrewarding or overfilled with responsibilities that keep us far too busy and fragment our sense of life's essential unity. Somewhere inside all the activities that comprise our daily life are blessings of one sort or another which make our lives rich with meaning. But we often have to hunt for them and sometimes the list we may have made can later seem a bit remote from what happens to us during an ordinary run-of-the-mill day. You may need to hunt down the blessings in your life in order to affirm them. You might find a simple event such as a stranger who smiled at you in the supermarket and made you feel noticed, or a child who suddenly ran up to hug you and reaffirm love. Whatever you find in this chase after the good and glad, write it down and pin it up on the wall and in your heart. Affirmations of love, hope, faith, joy and even foolishness all help us feel life is worth living.

Here is a list to inspire you. See how many blessings each of these reminds you of:

Love	Relationships	Thoughtfulness
Prosperity	Work	Appreciation of others
Healing	Sex	Independence
Health	Intuition	Patience
Capacity to feel	Confidence	Mother
Father	Sister/Brother	Friend

To count your blessings and get some balance between the up and down sides of your life is to enter the Gateway of Affirmation. It does not matter how young or old you are or what the state of your life is in the world's eyes at this moment.

The ultimate affirmation

The supreme affirmation is to believe in the existence of the Holy and to give thanks for its presence in your life. This is the greatest of all acts of thanksgiving because it affirms your oneness to all life and to the universe itself. It is a faith in the sacred that is not just of one moment in your spiritual life but the very climate in which you live. It embraces both the known and the hidden realms of your life, penetrates into the mystery of your being and opens realities beyond your reasoning. Until you yield yourself in this total way to the sacred, you will remain a stranger to yourself and excluded from the most meaningful depths of your own being. Your thanksgiving for this is a form of praise and adoration sung by the soul. It is the greatest of blessings.

THE NINTH
GATEWAY

Prayer –
The way of talking with God

The Gateway of Prayer is a practical way of creating harmony between our spiritual consciousness and the demands of living in the everyday world. It is a way open to everyone. Prayer stills the heart and gives you time and space in which to reconcile these two forces in your life. It puts some balance into your daily life so that you do not continue to separate your spirit, mind and body, but can treat them as the undivided self that makes you fully human. Prayer helps you recognise your wholeness by putting you in touch with how you really feel, and helping you to focus on love. To pray helps resolve your conflicting material and spiritual impulses. You can talk to God about your dilemma.

Prayer is the language of our spiritual quest. It is the voice of our soul. To pray is to be naked before the unknown. It is to admit that in spite of all the great accomplishments of our humanity, we still have a dimension that seeks this mysterious realm, which for lack of a better word we may call *God*. No matter what you pray about, your prayers always have hope in them, for you are declaring your trust in unseen powers to help your life. You are admitting that you alone do not and cannot control every aspect of your life, that there are forces in life which shape your destiny. In praying, you are asking for these forces to be benign and for a unity of self that is both personal and cosmic. You are hoping for a peaceful and fulfilled future no matter where you stand at this moment in time.

Who do you pray to?

Does there have to be someone out there listening to your prayers? It is worth pausing here to consider where you stand at the moment in terms of your concept of God. Otherwise any confusion you have could block the Gateway of Prayer for you.

Since God has no gender and is the God of a thousand names, you can take your pick of the many ways to envision the Holy. If the idea of some great Father in Heaven figure works for you, then fine. You might like the idea of a Mother God better. If Christ is what you see when you think of God, then your heart is already unfolding. If the words, 'There is no God but God' from the Qur'an, form on your lips when you think of God then you are already at prayer.

If you are keen on spirituality but aren't sure where you stand about God, this quick review of some of the main ideas of God may serve to clarify your thoughts: it is possible to view God as the essence of things; as the divine connection between things; as a power that can light up the soul; as the divine in everyone and everything; as the holy spirit; as the creator/destroyer like Shiva; as the Mother Goddess; as the Father of the universe; as incarnations in avatars like Jesus Christ; and as manifestations in gurus and other holy men and women. The Buddhist view of God is that there is no supreme creator because the world rises and declines in an eternal cycle. Christians see God as having three forms –

Father, Son and Holy Spirit. In Judaism God is seen as King of the Universe, the ultimate Father to be cleaved to and obeyed. For Muslims there is one all-powerful Creator. Hindus worship God in one or more forms from a large pantheon of gods and goddesses. The pantheistic view is that God and the universe are identical, implying that God has neither personality nor transcendence but exists in everything and, thus, takes all forms.

Unless you are committed to a particular religion, you probably see yourself as believing in this or that bit of one of the above areas of thought about how you define God and what God means to you. This is just as valid a place to be when you pray as any other because it is impossible for most people to define God. This is because defining God means trying to explain the most intimate of all relationships. It is a love affair between your soul and the unknown universal force of all life. Both of these invisible existences are full of hidden mysteries and meaning. We want to think about God, to discuss, argue, claim, disown, laugh at, cry for God, and finally perhaps just take it on trust that our instincts are right – that somewhere and somehow there is something we can call God.

The Japanese poet, Ariwara Narihira (825–80), told the story of a certain army captain who glimpsed a fair maiden's face through the curtains of a passing carriage. The soldier composed a poem to her, wanting to know who she was. I think the maiden's reply is equally true of the idea that it is necessary to define God:

> To know or not to know –
>
> Why should we make
>
> This vain distinction?
>
> This deep longing
>
> Alone is love's beacon.

This not an evasion or an easy way out of any dilemma we may have about understanding God, because it allows us to move forward in our spiritual pilgrimage. That is what is important. We can get on with practising a sacred life and, through the values and meanings we discover, perhaps one day realise ourselves as whole *and* holy. Praying helps us get to that goal of the inner self.

How strong is your faith?

At a dinner party recently a forty-something woman sitting next to me started talking about going to church. It seemed to me that what she said might apply to many people today. She declared herself a Christian. 'But I don't believe in God,' she told me. 'I do try to live a Christian life and to put into practise what Jesus taught, and I even sometimes go to church. You know – Christmas and Easter.' She told me about her struggle to live a moral and upright life and felt that made her a Christian. I asked her why she bothered to call herself a Christian if there was no God. Why not follow the example set by any other famously good man or woman – after all there are many in history to choose from besides Jesus. She was not pleased by my reply. Yet many people living in a Christian manner, with a childhood background of church services and stories about Jesus, think that this makes them a Christian. Can someone claim to be a follower of Christ and yet not believe in God? Could you claim to be a Muslim and not believe in God? Could you practise Native American spirituality and not believe in the Great Father? The answer for most people would be a resounding *no!* But is this judgement right? I am not so sure.

The woman sitting next to me at the dinner party may live out a life of love and kindness that more glorifies God than me, because even with my professions of faith, my churchgoing, and my baptismal claims on Christ, I may have forgotten those words of the Apostle James that 'faith without acts is dead'. (James 2:17).

So on the one hand a lot of people act in a Christian manner but do not have any real belief in God. Others have religious faith without the actions of love that need to go with it. In such matters of the spirit, people like the woman at the dinner party may give us much moral support through their example of living a life where *doing the right thing* is the guiding light.

However, nice as this social virtue may be, you cannot depend on it if it arises from the prompting of your ego and your senses, for these are liable to spring not from love but from your desires and self-importance. If you believe that you alone have the wisdom of the ages; that you alone may best judge the good and evil in life; that whatever your spirit may be, it marches to the tunes you decide to play, in effect you have separated yourself from God – never mind the name you give to what you say you are – be it Christian, Muslim, Hindu or whatever. The ego has taken charge of how you run your life and this is a barrier between you and God. The nature of living the sacred lies in your awareness of the presence of the holy in your life and not in how you define it.

Ask yourself if your being a seeker of the sacred depends on the support or devotion of those surrounding you? Does the strength of your trust in God depend only on the pronouncements of those religious figures you hold in esteem? Does your practice of prayer depend on the support and encouragement of others or on having everybody live up to your expectations? If you answer *yes* to these questions, your belief in a spiritual life is too fragile. It could be easily destroyed by your failure to live up to the standards you set yourself. You have not fully awakened the spiritual power at work within you. You have put your trust in the passing things of humanity and not in the life-renewing energy that is God. Prayer is a way to keep your dialogue with this eternal force going in the midst of personal problems, demands on your time, the seeming chaos and destruction in the world around you, lack of love in the actions of others, and all the arguments about God which are hindrances to the pilgrimage of your soul. A place

where we can all meet, no matter how we define our beliefs and
no matter what the success or failure of our ordinary life, is in a
state of prayer.

So where is God then?

I believe God is everywhere. Inside, outside and in between.
Substance and shadow. Visible and invisible. But I like best where
the little red hen thinks God is. She throws back her head every
time she drinks some water so as to look up and thank God. So
God is *up there* as well. Like the little red hen, we never think God
is *down there*. With a technological future that appears likely one
day to take us beyond the stars, heaven as we used to know it seems
increasingly a rather doubtful location for God's home. But then
it is said God has many mansions.

The great master of Sufism and theologian of Islamic doctrine,
Najm al Din Kubra (1145–1221), declared that the journey to
God is an inward one. God is inside us as that most radical of
Christian mystics, Meister Eckhart (*c.*1260–1328), would have it:
'One should not apprehend God nor consider Him outside one-
self, but as our own and as what is in ourselves.' (*Meister Eckhart:
The Essential Sermons*).

This being so, then everything that exists in the macrocosm
also exists within each of us, thus all the cosmos and all eternity
exists inside us. Your inner journey, like God, has no limit and no
one place. Al Din Kubra put it this way,

> Know that the lower soul, the Devil, and the Angel,
> the higher soul, are not external to you. You are
> they. So too, Earth and the Divine Throne of Being
> are not located outside, nor Paradise, Hell, Life or
> Death. All these exist in you, as you will realise once
> you have accomplished your journey to God and
> become pure.

Thus, all realms of existence are found within us. Here is the true dwelling place of God. You are, indeed, a holy temple.

When and where do you pray?

Since prayer is about your relationship with God, it presupposes communication from both sides. You pray to God in spoken or unspoken thoughts, and God listens and sometimes answers you. For most people God's communications are intuitive ones, sometimes so clear in the mind that the person praying feels they are spoken words. At other times, while nothing is heard with the heart, you may still feel that something is being said to you. I find I often get my reply via other people – maybe complete strangers – I meet after praying, whose words go straight to my heart. Praying brings inner stillness and in this stillness we may better understand what we are really praying about.

You can pray anytime and anywhere. You do not have to be in a church or a lovely natural setting. These may inspire you, but they are not necessary. Edmund Jones, a monk of Turvey Abbey, once said that he could pray even when in the bathroom, because it was your intentions that made where you were sacred enough for prayer. This may sound rather improper and not quite nice – but God is with you everywhere and what counts is that you pray, never mind where or when. Think of praying as the lighting of a candle which brightens up the soul. Does it matter where you light that candle?

What is happening when you pray?

When people pray they think what is important is that God should hear what they are saying, so they worry a lot about the form and content of their prayers. But the function of prayer is to arouse your natural human tendency to enter a divine or numinous state. Prayer both arouses this yearning and expresses it when you pray. Recently a young woman with three pre-school-age children told me that she had prayed from her heart in the most sincere fashion for years, yet always felt there was a space inside her still waiting to be fulfilled – and not by another pregnancy. Praying made her feel better, but it never quite satisfied this deep emptiness. Then one day it changed. She explained that she had prayed *only* for God's will in her life – just that and nothing more.

> Suddenly there was this sense that this space inside
> me was at last filled, that something had happened
> to make me feel so whole and so full of joy. I was
> really happy. I felt so glad for my children and myself
> and . . . everybody! It was as if God was there, right
> there with me. I guess it was my soul that got filled
> up!

So the function of prayer is partly to awaken and partly to express a sense of divine reality. It makes your soul the star on the stage of your enacting and creative self. Søren Kierkegaard (1813–55), a philosopher whose concerns were primarily spiritual, wrote: 'The true relation in prayer is not when God hears what is prayed for, but when the person praying continues to pray until he or she is the one who hears, who hears what God wills.'

When you pray you stand alone before God in the nakedness of your true self. You need to throw aside your ego like an old shirt: in prayer you annihilate this self-serving dimension of yourself. You seek your hidden self, the heart of your own nature, which is at once both earthly and eternal. You are seeking nothing less than the presence and will of God. Mohammed the Prophet told us to adore God as if we see him for, if we do not see him, he nevertheless sees us. So when you pray God is present no matter what your experience may be.

Our prayers bring our most intimate thoughts into full consciousness and announce our heart's desires to God. When we ask God to lead us on 'the right path', this is the path of sacred living which leads to the perfection of our spirit, mind and body in all Creation. If we pray for such union, God says, 'My servant will receive that for which she asks.' And this must surely be the real answer to all prayers because this is the ultimate message of hope, forgiveness and love. It is for this reason that throughout history saints, sages and ordinary women and men in all lands and in all walks of life have made prayer the centre of their lives. Our prayers endow our lives with the spiritual history of our ancestors and lay down a welcome for our children in times yet to come. Our prayers become an act of virtue and God's reward is grace. We are redeemed by the spirit.

Every day of your life you are asked in a thousand ways to become a slave of something. There are lots of golden idols to worship – possessions, power, politics, money, fame. Above all these your ego sits on a throne of your own making. It gets more demanding with each passing year of your life. It dictates the mantra of your daily life and repeats it endlessly in your head: 'I am important! I am important! I am important!' So when you call on God in your prayers, bow down or kneel and make a gentle act of respect. Do not pretend anything but say like a child, 'God, this is just me. Open my heart, please.' In this way you submit to the eternal. In this way you trust God to raise up your soul. You cease to be a slave of illusion and become freed in the spirit.

The language of prayer

Our prayer is always a language of seeking and it has the sweet taste of hope in it. The words we use when we pray may spring from deep within us or they may be the words of a written prayer. These words are symbols we use to look through and beyond their ordinary meaning to the unknown they point to. They direct our minds to the mysterious reality of God. The form of our prayer and the nature of the words we use will be shaped by our purpose – adoration, confession, thanksgiving, petition or intercession.

Adoration

This kind of prayer acknowledges the over-arching reality of God in all things. We express how insignificant we feel in the scheme of the universe, and our sense of the significance of being given life. These are prayers of delight. Here is such a prayer by St Symeon Styllites of the Orthodox tradition. Focus your prayer by imagining as you begin that you are inviting God into your life – to come to you in all forms of mystery and glory.

Come, true light. Come, life eternal.

Come, hidden mystery. Come, treasure with name.

Come, reality beyond all words.

Come, person beyond all understanding.

Come, rejoicing without end.

Come, light that knows no evening.

Come, unfailing expectation of the saved.

Come, raising of the fallen. Come, resurrection of the dead.

Come, all powerful, for unceasingly you create, refashion and change all things by your will alone.

Come, invisible whom none may touch and handle.

Come, for you continue always unmoved, yet at every instant you are wholly in movement; you draw near to us who lie in hell, yet you remain higher than the heavens.

Come, for your name fills our hearts with longing and is ever on our lips; yet who you are and what your nature is, we cannot say or know.

Come, Alone to the alone.

Come, for you are yourself the desire that is within me.

Come, my breath and my life.

Come, the consolation of my humble soul.

Come, my joy, my glory, my endless delight.

Confession

Our prayers of confession spring from a feeling that we have some-how been estranged from God. This mainly happens when we become aware of our failure to love. Our confession is a cry for healing and reconciliation between the two forces of our nature – the one which likes the world and the other which yearns for God. We confess not only our own failings but the collective ones of humanity. Hence, a prayer of confession is about penitence. The psychologist Carl Jung (1875–1961) pleaded, 'If only people could realise what an enrichment it is to find one's own guilt.' He claimed such a discovery gives us a sense of honour and spiritual dignity, because it acknowledges not just our own failings and sins but makes known to us that we too share in the crimes of all men and women. Our enrichment comes about because in acknowledging this collective guilt we also share in humanity's estrangement from a life of true harmony with God. It is just such a harmony that we all seek when we desire to become pure and cleansed in our hearts.

Begin your prayer of confession by meditating on how impor-tant loving is. If you feel you have neglected to love someone or have not been loving in a particular situation, confess this to your-self, bringing it into full awareness. Remind yourself then that not to love is to draw away from God in others. What you want is a pure heart which is a dwelling place for the eternal.

Here is a prayer of confession from an African schoolgirl:

> O great chief, light a candle in my heart, that I may
> see what is therein, and sweep the rubbish from your
> dwelling place.

The direct simplicity of her prayer is echoed in Psalm 51 which
you can use at either the beginning or end of your prayer of confession:

> A pure heart create for me, O God,
>
> put a steadfast spirit within me.
>
> Do not cast me away from your presence,
>
> nor deprive me of your holy spirit.

Thanksgiving

When we thank God, we express our faith and our gratitude which
strengthens our sense of dependence on God. We give thanksgiving for what's enjoyable in our lives – the abundance of blessings
that even in the midst of tribulations we can find if we only look.
This is summed up in the following Chinese saying: 'Have mercy
on me, O Beneficent one, I was angered for I had no shoes. Then
I met a man who had no feet.' The character of a prayer of thanksgiving is gladness.

This prayer from the Kikuyu people of Kenya (quoted in *The
Oxford Book of Prayers*, 1985) is a good one to launch a time of
prayerful gratitude. Let it open you to all the 'glorious gifts' in your
life. There are many that will come into your mind no matter what
your situation – good health, a decent job, a roof over your head,
the trees in the park, the warm sun on your face, the food you eat,
the gift of your talents.

O my father, Great Elder,

I have no words to thank you,

But with your deep wisdom

I am sure that you can see

How I value your glorious gifts.

Perhaps you are in ill-health or homeless, even hungry or in prison – how can you be glad? Begin to pray with these few words from the Qur'an: 'Things overwhelm me: come to my help' (Noah's prayer in The Moon 54:10), and then look into yourself and know that you can be glad of your uniqueness in this universe and the fact that you belong to God – personally, intimately and with love. That above all else is what should bring you to pray in thanksgiving.

Petition and Intercession

'God help us!' sums up prayers of petition and intercession. The prayer attributed to Mohammed on entering the mosque was this same cry: 'Open to me the doors of Thy mercy'. Tradition also holds that the Prophet said, 'Petition is the weapon of the believer and the pillar of faith and the light of heaven and earth.'

   We are asking God to intervene and help human life. It may be prayers to end a war, to help the homeless, to heal a loved one. Some people find that they have difficulty praying for distant events – a refugee crisis or the victims of a natural disaster – but are able to pray for those they know – family, friends and people at work, which is just fine because both near and far there are those who need our prayers. The list of what we could pray to God to influence is nearly endless because we are under constant attack from immediate situations and distant circumstances which affect our health, our thoughts and the state of our spiritual life.

When we ask God for something we are like a child again, putting all our trust and faith in a higher authority and admitting to our powerlessness, inadequacy, and need to be helped. In such prayers of petition and intercession we begin to break down the mistrust that our adult life has brought us – all the suspicion and scepticism about our own motives and those of other people. Our child-like simplicity and open trust illuminates the depths of our personality and stimulates healing to begin in us. Our inner child lives again in the playground of innocence and trust which is the domain of God. Our fullest physical and mental resources have been activated. We are no longer in the state of distress which makes us physically and spiritually ill, but in a state of peace where healing may take place. The energy within us flows out to meet an energy that comes from God. This mysterious spiritual force can bring direct results – the lame walk, the blind see and the anxiety of the heart disappears. God is with us. Our prayers are answered.

This short English prayer from the sixteenth century covers most of the elements of petition:

> Into the hands of your blessed protection and
> unlimited mercy, O God, I commend this day my
> soul and my body with all their faculties, powers and
> actions, asking you to be always with me, to direct,
> sanctify, and lead me in the ways of your laws, and in
> the works of your commandments that through your
> great protection, both now and forever, I may be
> preserved in my body and soul to serve you.

What can you ask for when you pray?

Can we ask for anything definite from God when we pray? Valerius, the Roman historian, tells us that the philosopher Socrates maintained that nothing further should be asked of the immortal gods save that they should give us good, and this on the grounds that they well knew what was best for each person, whereas we often ask in our prayers for that which it would be better not to have asked for. Positive answers to requests for power, prestige, riches, and even what may appear to be innocent desires have ruined many individuals and kingdoms.

Yet, when we pray we often do ask for things: Lord, give me that job! Oh, God, please let me have that new car! Come on, let me win the lottery! Such things are of the world and, as St Damascene and other holy men and women have often told us, a better way to prayer is to ask God for things which are fitting for us as individuals. The Apostle John said that we must worship in spirit and truth (NT 4.24). If your heart is on the passing things of this world and the ever-changing desires within you, then how can you claim your prayers are of a spiritual nature?

It would seem then that we ought to ask God for those virtues which benefit living a sacred life. One reason to do this is that the more our minds are occupied by ordinary desires, the more we will be aware of our failure to achieve them. We will not be uplifted. Even multimillionaires who can buy whatever they want are not immune from this spiritual affliction. A friend of mine, who is a freelance cook for the very wealthy, often tells me how unhappy her clients are. 'These women I work for,' she says, 'they have so much and yet they worry all the time about little things. They get so depressed!'

What matters is not what can be seen – the things of this world which decay and pass away and never fill the soul with joy. What matters in the long run is what is unseen – the love in our lives, the happiness we create in others, the bliss of knowing our children are safe, the kindness of a stranger, the pleasure of a friend's companionship. These are the unseen but eternal things about which we should talk with God. So why bother to ask for this or that? Why stumble about in the mud of your own desiring? You can sum it all up this way when you pray: God, bring me what

I need and bid me what I am. Make no possession my master save Nature itself.

Can we pray for our enemies? Should we hope, like some ideal Christian, to turn the other cheek and ignore the affronts to us? I think praying for those who wish us harm or treat us unjustly is a really hard thing to do. It is a work of real love. Some of us are lucky enough to live in liberty but millions of people are crushed by evil. They cry out with the Psalmist (35:17), 'O Lord, how long will you look on? Come to my rescue! Save my life from these raging beasts, my soul from these lions.' Whether we face evil personally or just watch some appalling crime news on television, we are aware of injustice and cruelty. How can we then pray for anyone who violates others? We cannot *love* such faults in others but we can try to pray for their perfection in God. St Thomas Aquinas (1225–74) tells us to ask for our enemy's union with God in love. This defeats all evil.

When you pray in this way for those who wish you harm you turn your thoughts to God as consummate love, and this brings an easing of your anger and hurt. In this way you may find a measure of peace and a way out of despair. Ask yourself how else the few survivors of the Holocaust could find any peace. Read the testimony of those who have suffered torture. See how they have not permitted evil to take up residence in their souls no matter how terrible the aggression against their minds and bodies. How else can we deal with evil except to lift our spirit towards God? From there you can begin to see the real nature of evil, which is the absence of the holy. You can begin to pray for its transformation into love, which is the essence of the sacred and the pure of heart.

Shared Prayer

In most spiritual traditions there are shared rituals, including praying together. For Christians, the words of Jesus Christ bring them together: 'In truth I tell you once again, if two of you on earth agree to ask anything at all, it will be granted to you by my Father in heaven. For where two or three meet in my name, I am there among them.' (Matthew 18:19). In Native American spirituality, life itself is like a great song and sacred rituals include prayers chanted and danced together. These express the all-embracing and inherent harmony, peace and balance found in nature as Creation. What the Navajo call *hozhoni*. A return to such perfect harmony is sought in shared praying.

Shared prayer seems to fall into three forms. We may say aloud or sing together a prayer from memory or from a book. We can pray together in silence at the same time, which can help to create in us a powerful sense of holy presence. Finally, we can let prayers arise as they will from our hearts and form into words as we are assembled together. Holding hands when you pray together often strengthens the bonds of faith between believers.

All of these ways of praying together seem to help people. They remind us of our shared humanity and that others too yearn for the sacred and are seeking God. This witnessing can inspire us. It tells us that others too suffer from their failures and cry out to be understood and forgiven. In this way we may be prompted to forget our self-concern and find love and compassion for others. When we hear someone else, particularly a stranger we don't know, speak of a pain or hope or spiritual desire that we similarly hold within ourselves, our heart is opened.

Together we can offer prayers of adoration, confession, thanksgiving, petition and intercession. Our failures and needs are admitted, our sense of love renewed, and our delight in life shared. We are helping each other to open up to God and joining St Augustine in his great cry to God: 'You are more deeply in me than I am in myself!'

Difficulties of prayer

One difficulty that many people experience about praying is that they seem to have no time to do it. It isn't that they don't want to pray, it is just that life is too busy. The best of intentions go astray.

You have to make time for prayer. Give five minutes a day to God – that may seem very little but just add it up over a year and you will have spent at least twenty-two hours in spiritual sanctuary. Think of all that calm and peace. Make it the same five minutes each day if you can, so it becomes a habit – perhaps when you first wake up in the morning. Let your first thoughts be of God. Keep it simple: 'Thanks be to God! I am alive for another day!' can be enough. It starts the day. It is a prayer.

What about the time you take to travel to work? On the train or bus, close your eyes, let your feelings come to the surface, and pray silently in the midst of all the busy world around you. Make your inner space an oasis of comfort. If you drive to work, give yourself five minutes to sit quietly after parking the car. For many people this is just about the only time when they are left alone and will not be interrupted – make the car a sanctuary. Do some spiritual recollection. Pray about yourself and the day ahead. Pray a little for someone at work that you know is having problems. Thank God and go on to work.

We can be too full of expectation about our prayers. We may feel like Molly, an old Irishwoman I knew, who confessed with sadness and frustration: 'Every Sunday I go to church and nothing happens. Every night I say my prayers and nothing ever happens then either.' But what did Molly expect from God? She didn't want miracles, mysterious voices, or to be touched by an angel. Molly just wanted *something* to happen when she prayed. Here she was, at the very end of a long life, and still no luck it seemed with God. No one had ever bothered to tell her that when she was drawn to pray it was God bringing her close, that God was already there before the first words had come from her heart and were sent to his ear. How else except with God's presence could she have found the faith to live a life of prayer? His answer had been to give her a life of trust and hope. When Molly thought over these things, she decided that God had given her something after all. Her praying became free of the hindrance of expectation. God had been there all the time.

When you pray, God has prompted you. He is already there, so do not wait upon anything but God's will. This clears up any kind of difficulty in prayer.

The habit of prayer

St Augustine wrote that it was no great thing to live long nor to live for ever, but it was indeed a great thing to *live*. Praying regularly helps us to remember that we have this great gift of life itself. This is a good place to start in your praying. Stupid as it may sound, many people do tend to forget that the most important thing is that they are actually *alive*. Depression, anxieties, worries over superficial things, inability to keep peace in family relationships, envy of others, feelings of sexual inadequacy, concerns about personal appearance – all these can drown out the inner voice that wants to say: 'Hey! If nothing else let's just be thankful to be alive!' Becoming aware of this helps to keep all those other passing concerns in perspective. It is, after all, just such a balance that we all need in order to live at peace in this fast-paced and stressful world. The next time you fret over your hair, complain you have nothing to wear, feel useless, or suffer from any of the many daily anxieties of life, read these words of Jesus Christ.

I am telling you not to worry about your life and
what you are to eat, nor about your body and what
you are to wear. Surely life is more than food, and
the body more than clothing! Look at the birds in

the sky. They do not sow or reap or gather into
barns; yet your heavenly Father feeds them. Are you
not worth much more than they are? Can any of
you, however much you worry, add one single cubit
to your span of life? And why worry about clothing?
Think of the flowers growing in the fields; they
never have to work or spin; yet I assure you that not
even Solomon in all his royal robes was clothed like
one of these. Now if that is how God clothes the
wild flowers growing in the fields which are there
today and thrown into the furnace tomorrow, will he
not much more look after you, you who have so
little faith? So do not worry; do not say, 'What are
we to eat? What are we to drink? What are we to
wear?' . . . Your heavenly Father knows you need . . .
all these things. Set your hearts on his kingdom first,
and on God's saving justice, and all these other
things will be given you as well. So do not worry
about tomorrow: tomorrow will take care of itself.
Each day has enough trouble of its own.

(Matthew 6:25–34)

These words help us honour a greater vision for our life than the
mere passing of our days in shallow concerns. They return us to a
balance between the ordinary and the spiritual. In this way we
may keep ourselves in a sacred place. From this sense of appreciation for just being alive, and with a renewed trust in the future, it
is an easy step to prayerful words of adoration, confession, thanksgiving, and petition.

Shaping up for prayer – praying with all of yourself

Prayer is not just an inner thing: when we pray we should be praying with our whole being, not just somewhere inside our head. No more organising yourself into compartments. No more fragmentation of self. This is not another business appointment, or an hour at the pre-school play group, or the time to phone your investment broker or your mother. This is God time. You are meeting up with the Big One, so you want all of yourself to be there – the ordinary

---

Physical preparation for prayer

Do thirty minutes moderate exercise each day if you are on retreat; ten minutes if you are at home. Walk briskly, rake some leaves in the garden, ride a bike if one is handy, polish some furniture, wash a car, or mop the floor. If briskly done, such exercise will burn up some calories too. It lessens stress and improves the function of your immune system. Prayer time is healing time.

Preparing for prayer if you are ill

If you are ill, you need to take special care in preparing for prayer. Pain can dominate us, lead us into a confusion of thoughts and feelings, and make us very angry with everybody, including God. When this happens our pain has made us despair, and this lack of hope is one of the few emotions that can suffocate the spirit. The way to our inner space simply locks up and hopelessness takes us over. Praying will calm you down, renew your hope, and so bring healing. It lets you visualise a future in which you will again be well.

Begin your praying by relaxing and letting go, as much as you can, of the pain and discomfort you are feeling. Focus on your breathing – imagine your breath going in and coming out evenly, gently, carefully. Let yourself slip into a meditative state.

---

part of you and the hidden part of you. You want your body in balance, your mind focused and not drifting about with desires and anxieties and you want to offer a heart full of love. Above all, you want to be truly yourself.

Preparing your body for prayer does not have to be some medieval religious exercise in self-deprivation – sackcloth and ashes, and gestures of self-denial. Simply doing some bodywork before you start praying will make you more attentive.

Fasting: Expressing your hunger for God

Religious and spiritual traditions have long affirmed that fasting is an important key that opens wide the Gateway of Prayer. Fasting for spiritual reasons is praying with the body, expressing a hunger only for God, and reaffirming the wholeness of yourself in spiritual action. When our fast has this spiritual intention, we are surrendering our pleasures, undergoing an act of purification, and expressing a number of spiritual things. These include penitence, thanksgiving and the rejection of gluttony.

Religious rituals often include observance of fasting. For example, on the Jewish day of Atonement, Yom Kippur; the Islamic tradition of fasting during daylight for the month of Ramadan; and the forty days of Lent when Christians are admonished to cut their consumption of food and drink, to give up something they enjoy eating, or to restrict their consumption of animal products. Fasting on such occasions is both an individual and a community ritual of purification. It clarifies the senses and purifies the body so that you may listen to God with your heart and discover your true self.

Jesus fasted in private and for the purpose of prayer. He shows that solitude is the natural companion of fasting and that this withdrawal and purifying of the self serves to orientate you to God.

It is a way of removing the distractions and hindrances of our bodily needs. It is a practise that, done correctly and *in keeping with your state of health,* offers a strengthening of the soul. Fasting for reasons of mere fashion is as sad as gluttony. It can also spring from the kind of personal anxiety which results in eating disorders.

Fasting for spiritual reasons is incomprehensible without prayer. In spiritual terms it is meaningless unless you are aware that you are fasting out of love and that your giving up of a natural desire to eat and drink is for a higher cause. When you fast, you call a halt to ordinary urges and the pleasuring of self. Fasting will teach you much about your human appetites. To abstain is to draw back from these appetites and to consider again how you are balancing your life. It is the sacrifice of a little pleasure in order to get a focus on important questions in your life – those questions which can remain with you even though you may be successful by the world's standards: 'Who am I? What is the meaning of my life? Where am I really going?'

Fasting is a form of asceticism, the practice of a self-discipline. It is only one aspect of a whole range of ascetic spiritual practises. Others include celibacy as an expression of sexual reservation; putting others' needs before our own; and choosing simplicity over satiety when it comes to possessions. The real imperative behind asceticism for spiritual reasons is to focus our whole attention on the sacred, to which we want all the urgencies of our hungers to turn. Our self-denial is nothing unless our motivation is to seek God.

What does fasting involve?

Fasting is the partial or total avoidance of food and drink, except for water, for a certain length of time. Modified versions of fasting are diets restricted to a few foods only or just fruit juices. Most people have reserves of fat stored in their body, so there is no question that fasting means starving yourself. However, fasting does result in deep changes in the body and the beginning of a variety of self-healing detoxification and repair processes.

If this is so, why don't more people fast? We live in an age of over-consumption in which the idea of putting something *into* our body in order to cope with life is still the dominant wisdom of the age. We want the easy way out and this idea of the quick fix affects most of our thinking, including how we handle our spiritual life. Fasting means denial, and we live in a culture of self-indulgence.

Fasting also involves commitment and accepting responsibility for yourself, which are essential virtues in practising a sacred

---

Warning

If you decide to undertake a fast, read the following advice *carefully*. If you have any doubts, consult a health professional about it.

1. Fasting should NOT be undertaken if you are under eighteen years of age or over sixty, pregnant, or suffering from any illness, without prior consultation with a medical doctor.

2. Do not fast beyond forty-eight hours if you are emaciated, pregnant, menstruating, diabetic, suffering from any kind of kidney or liver disease, or taking prescription drugs. If any fast is taken for longer than forty-eight hours it is strongly recommended that a qualified health care professional be consulted and supervision ensured and available.

3. Under no circumstances should fasting last more than three days without supervision.

4. Water must be drunk liberally at all times to maintain correct body fluid levels.

5. Fasting is not advisable for anyone with an eating disorder or suffering from any form of mental health problem.

Common side effects of fasting

Some or all of the following side effects can occur when you fast. The last two will probably continue during the fast, the others should disappear after the first thirty-six hours or so.

1. Headaches (at start of fast).

2. Insomnia (at start of fast).

3. A coated tongue and sometimes nausea.

4. Light-headedness and dizziness especially if you get up quickly after lying down.

5. Increased body odour and dry skin.

6. Muscle aches in limbs.

7. A feeling of being colder.

8. Not hungry after the first day of fast.

9. Less bowel function activity.

life. Fasting is a revitalising experience for most people and an ancient tradition for healing the whole person. The use of fasting as a therapeutic technique is common in Germany and Scandinavia and is becoming popular as an alternative health approach in Britain and the USA. Research has shown fasting can offer benefits in a range of diseases, for example in the treatment of rheumatoid arthritis and other auto-immune diseases, including some forms of kidney disease. The body does a lot of self-repairing given half a chance. The evidence is fairly strong that restricting calorie intake but maintaining a complete nutrient intake has anti-aging potential for mammals. By slowing down your basic metabolic rate, burning energy slower, and reducing toxicity levels in the body, there is less free radical activity to cause tissue damage. Fasting once in a while might mean a longer life. Done as a spiritual exercise, it means you are *really* concentrating on developing a spiritual life.

A weekend fast

This is a water only fast. Symptoms of hunger will quickly disappear unless you decide to drink fruit juice as well as water, when a sense of hunger will remain with you. The day before you begin your fast, cut down on your food. Eat fruit and salads. Eat very lightly in the evening, perhaps only some fruit. Start your fast on Friday night and end it on Sunday evening.

1. Drink at least three litres of *pure* water each day during this fast – that means purified, still spring water. Do not drink tap water, which is chlorinated.

2. No hot baths, no soaking in the water.

3. Do *not* work during your fast.

4. Don't watch TV or listen to the radio.

5. Practise deep breathing, relaxation and meditation.

6. Let your spirit rise up in you as your desire for food, drink and amusements of the mind lessen. Your mind will become clearer, your body lighter. You are saying to yourself: 'I love you.' You are opening your heart.

7. Take very gentle exercise during the weekend, such as stretching and a little walking – no games or sports or extended rambles. Conserve your energy.

8. Expect some or all of the side effects listed above. Do not take any aspirin or paracetamol if you get a headache or aches and pains. These will pass.

9. If you are addicted to any food or substance like chocolate or coffee, you may get withdrawal symptoms such as a slight headache or a feeling of uneasiness: discipline yourself to resist these desires.

If the whole business is making you distressed then stop and try it some other time when you feel up to it.

The way a fast is ended is as important as how it is conducted. *Maintain your pure water intake for four days after your fast.*

The first thing you eat after this forty-eight hour fast should be a glass of fresh fruit or vegetable juice, preferably raw, diluted half-and-half with pure water and sipped very slowly during the morning. Drink two or three more glasses of this diluted juice during the day. In the evening steam a few vegetables and eat these *without salt or other condiments*. The next day eat fresh fruit and some vegetable soup. Add low fat yogurt or a small green salad to this menu for your meal on the third day. On the fourth day, eat normally.

Unfolding the heart: a week of prayers

The following prayers are drawn from many religious and spiritual traditions, all based on a God-centred spirituality. They ask for your life to be one of love, peace and unity. Before each prayer there is a short note about it to help you meditate, before you begin, on the meaning and intent behind the words of the prayer.

These seven days are designed to get you into a daily habit of prayer, to deliberately make time for your interior life. You will be putting aside the concerns of the world and seeking your true self. This is the practice of the presence of God in your life.

Remember that when we move away from our selfish concerns and give ourselves over to a greater love in prayer, we are aligning our energies and deepest self with all existence – our fellow humans, the creatures and plants around us, the deep earth below us and the lovely stars and unknown worlds above us. The desire of your soul is to be embraced by the divine will, to realise a unity not only within yourself but with all Creation. Simplicity is the key. Let your interior vision unfold to ever-widening perceptions.

When you say these prayers silently or aloud let the real feelings, thoughts and visions that are in your heart come alive. Bring them to the surface of your consciousness. Some will be of love, many of anger, others of hope and pleading, a few of deep pain. Bring all these to God and then *listen*.

Prayers to say every day

When you wake each morning, open your heart at once to God. Let nothing occupy your mind. Let your body rest in this peacefulness. Allow your mind to slip into the garden of your soul.

Here are two of the most profound prayers ever given to humanity. Both are considered to have been divinely revealed. They gather together all the intentions of all prayers. They proclaim faithfulness and hope. They open the heart to God in words of love.

Al-Fâtiha: the opening prayer of the Qur'an

This prayer comes at the beginning of the daily formal prayers of the Islamic faith and was given by Mohammed, the Prophet of God. The passage embodies the essence of Islam, which is the oneness of God.

IN THE NAME OF ALLAH

THE COMPASSIONATE

THE MERCIFUL

Praise be to Allah, Lord of the Creation,

The Compassionate, the King of Judgement-day!

You alone we worship, and to You alone we pray for help.

Guide us to the straight path

The path of those whom You have favoured,

Not of those who have incurred Your wrath,

Nor of those who have gone astray.

(Qur'an, The Exordium)

The Lord's Prayer

This prayer was given by Jesus Christ with these words: Your Father already knows what you need before you ask him. This, then, is how you should pray:

Our Father in heaven,

May your holy name be honoured;

may your kingdom come;

may your will be done on earth as it is in heaven.

Give us today the food we need.

Forgive us the wrongs we have done,

as we forgive the wrongs that others have done to us.

Do not lead us to temptation,

but save us from evil.

(Matthew 6:8–13)

Night prayers

Our last prayers at night, the ones we murmur before we leave our consciousness of this world, should leave all worry and anxiety with God. Be like the boy in Dylan Thomas's *A Child's Christmas in Wales*: 'I said some words to the close and holy darkness, and then I slept.'

These few words of night prayer place all your trust in God:

God grant me a quiet night and a perfect end.

Day 1: A prayer of acknowledgement

This prayer is from the Celtic Christian tradition and is inspired by the answer Moses got when he asked God his name and God replied, 'I am . . . this is my name forever'. (Exodus 3:14, 15)

I am the wind which blows over the sea;

I am the wave of the ocean; I am the murmur of the billows;

I am a tear of the Sun; I am the fairest of plants;

I am a wild boar in valour; I am a salmon in the water;

I am a lake in the plain; I am a word of wisdom;

I am the arrow of truth which gives victory;

I am the God which creates in humanity the fire of thought;

Who will enlighten each question if not I?

Day 2: A prayer for help

Written by Jacob Astley in the seventeenth century, this prayer asks for help in getting through an ordinary day in spite of all our human failings. This is a good prayer for anyone who lives a life in which there are too many things to do, too much work to finish and too many people to see, meet, and deal with. I think of this as the 'Busy People' prayer.

Help me today to realise that you will be speaking to
me through the events of the day, through people,
through things, and through all Creation.

Give me ears, eyes and heart to perceive you,
however veiled your presence may be.

Give me insight to see through the exterior of things
to the interior truth.

Give me your spirit of discernment.

O, God, you know how busy I must be this day.

If I forget you, do not forget me!

Day 3: A prayer of praise

To celebrate God is to welcome all Creation on this earth and in
the worlds which only falling stars may find. We proclaim through
our praise a vision of the holiness of life in all its diversity. We reaffirm the majesty of the continuous oneness of the universe. Our
awe in the face of this beautiful secret may find the theme for all
prayers in these few words: 'From all eternity, O Lord, you are.'
(Psalm 93)

This is Psalm 148 which proclaims cosmic praise from the
whole of Creation to the eternal glory of God.

Praise the Lord from the heavens,

praise him in the heights.

Praise him, all his angels,

praise him, all his host!

Praise him, sun and moon,

praise him, shining stars.

Praise him, highest heavens

and the waters above the heavens.

Let them praise the name of the Lord.

He commanded: they were made.

He fixed them for ever,

gave a law which shall not pass away.

Praise the Lord from the earth,

sea creatures and all oceans,

fire and hail, snow and mist,

stormy winds that obey his word;

All mountains and hills, all fruit trees and cedars,

beasts, wild and tame,

reptiles and birds on the wing;

all earth's kings and peoples,

earth's princes and rulers;

young men and maidens,

old men together with children.

Let them praise the name of the Lord

for he alone is exalted.

The splendour of his name

reaches beyond heaven and earth.

Alleluia!

Day 4: A prayer for oneness

The main founder of the Baha'i faith was Baha'ullah (1817–92),
who taught appreciation of all faiths, because there is a oneness of
all humans, a oneness of all religions and a oneness of all prophets.
He said, 'The religion of God is love and unity. Make it not the
cause of enmity and dissension.' Here is a prayer from the Baha'i
tradition asking for mercy and wisdom as you stand alone before
God.

> O Thou Who art the Lord of all names and the
> Maker of the Heavens! I beseech Thee by them
> Who are the Day-springs of Thine invisible Essence,
> the Most Exalted, the All Glorious, to make of my
> prayer a fire that will burn away the veils which
> have shut me out of Thy beauty, and a light that will
> lead me unto the ocean of Thy Presence.
>
> (Baha'i Prayers, The Baha'i Publishing Trust)

Day 5: A prayer of blessing

It is really true that if we count up our blessings, including all the
tiny ones, we will have an abundance. This bundle of good things
will outweigh all the worries and moans and bad times that make
us so often imagine life is a dead end. Just stopping for a moment
to give thanks for the day will lift your spirits and make you feel
better. Try it. It works.

This simple prayer, attributed to a London hospital porter of
earlier this century, may not be long or elegant or famous, but it
says it all for me. Maybe for you too?

> Good morning, Guv'nor, and thank you.

Day 6: A prayer for grace

It is essential for people of the Hindu faith to perform the actions of living which come from their own evolution of self. In the Bhagavadgita, the best known Hindu sacred scripture, the instruction is: 'Do your allotted duty. Action is indeed superior to inaction. Even the survival of your body would not be possible without action.' Our allotted duty may be seen as those actions which enable us to fully develop our natural self, to live in a state of grace with other people and with nature, and to enjoy an abiding link between our self-consciousness and our consciousness of the Cosmic. In this way the actions of your life serve to achieve awareness of God, and you will be acting in a way which is not contrary to the unity of life. You will be unfolding your true self. So in this prayer by St Francis of Assisi you are asking to be made an instrument of God's will so that all your actions serve to make you a person of compassion.

> Lord, make me an instrument of your peace.
>
> Where there is hatred, let me sow love;
>
> Where there is injury, pardon;
>
> Where there is doubt, faith;
>
> Where there is despair, hope;
>
> Where there is darkness, light;
>
> Where there is sadness, joy.
>
> O Divine Master, grant that I may not so much seek
>
> To be consoled, as to console,
>
> To be understood, as to understand,
>
> To be loved, as to love.

For it is in giving that we receive;

It is in pardoning that we are pardoned;

It is in dying that we are born to eternal life.

> (*St Francis of Assisi: His life and writings*, Thomas of
> Celano trans. L. Sherley-Price, 1959)

Day 7: A prayer of healing

Healing through spiritual means is an important aspect of living a sacred life. When we are ill or in physical pain it is very hard to focus on anything else. When the disaster of a really serious illness strikes us we are likely to say, 'Why me? What have I done to deserve this!' Many people first become angry and resentful, but this passes in time for most. As they gradually accept what has happened to them, they begin to feel hope for the future. It is right that we should hope for our life. Hope works at a deep level of our inner self, affecting the spirit, mind and body. It is a positive force for physical and emotional healing.

If you are not yourself ill or in suffering, be assured someone you know is. They may have a physical illness or be in mourning for the loss of a loved one. They may be depressed, lonely, anxious over their employment, or trying to resolve a failed relationship. Somewhere there is an unknown prisoner who despairs of justice. Each of these people will be in a place of pain and in need of hope. Pray for them. This action will in turn increase your own sense of hope for your own future.

When we live in hope, it is a signal that we are living the sacred for we desire not to be separated from God who is the well-spring of hope. We reaffirm that in the continuous oneness of Creation there is but one body and one spirit. It is in this way that just as your own suffering is part of you so the suffering of others is part of you. A thirteenth-century poem by the Persian Sufi mystic, Rumi, sums this up and serves as a point of meditation.

On the way you may want to look back, or not, but if you can say 'There's nothing ahead,' there will be nothing there.

Stretch your arms and take hold of the cloth of your clothes with both hands. The cure for pain is in the pain. Good and bad are mixed. If you don't have both, you don't belong with us.

When one of us gets lost, is not here, he must be inside us. There's no place like that anywhere in the world.

(*The Essential Rumi*,
trans. Coleman Banks, Harper San Francisco, 1995)

The following prayer for healing is based on prayers transmitted from Mohammed the Prophet and his companions. As you pray, give up your fear and loneliness, and hope for the future. At the end of this prayer ask in your own words for the healing you need.

Oh, God, heal me in my body; heal me in my hearing;

heal me in my seeing.

There is no God but you.

There is no God but you.

There is no God but you.

Oh, God I ask You for the good things,

and for performance of good deeds,

and avoidance of evil deeds, and for love of the unfortunate.

I ask you for Your love and the love of those who
love You,

and for the love of every deed

which brings me nearer to Your love,

and I ask You to turn towards me and to forgive me,

and to have mercy upon me.

Contemplation – The happiness of the perfected soul

There is a kind of prayer in which the mind does not function discursively but rests in the Divine. If words escape from the lips, they are few and whispered as if from the lover into the ear of the beloved. It involves continuously being with God. It is the happiness of the perfected soul.

John Joseph Suring was born in Bordeaux in 1600 and for most of his life he suffered from the many spiritual problems he found in himself and in others. Finally, when he was almost sixty, these things seemed to pass and he began to write down as spiritual teachings what had been revealed to him during those long, dark years of spiritual suffering. He insisted God must be loved in all things and explained what the happiness of a perfected soul was in this way: in our union with what is divine, we fill our hearts with God and hold dear the most desirable of good things. These good things are the experience of the fullness of God in all Creation from the littlest seed or grain of sand to the most enormous mountains and mysterious seas. We have a sense of Divine Majesty in all creatures and all matter.

It follows that the more we are living a sacred life, the more we are in conversation with God through our thoughts, deeds, words, prayers and love. The soul is led through this communion into peace and happiness. Surin tells us that in this contemplative state we are continuously immersed in the essence of the Holy,

> as it were in a deep pool of peace and love, the soul bathing herself in the light and fire of God like a fish in the sea. As the fish is born to the freedom of the whole ocean, and can swim wherever he will without let or hindrance, so the soul has the boundless immensity of God in which deliciously to lose herself at any moment.
>
> (*An Anthology of Mysticism*,
> ed. Paul de Jaegher, Burns & Oates, 1977)

The practice of deep contemplation is a very special prayer of the soul in love with God. St Teresa of Avila (1515–82) called it the prayer of quiet. She thought it almost a supernatural state because only God could bring it about in a person.

> This recollection of the soul makes itself felt largely through the satisfaction and peace which it brings to it, together with a very great joy and repose of the faculties and a most sweet delight.
>
> (*Selected Writings of St Teresa of Avila*,
> ed. William J. Doheny, Bruce Publishing, 1950)

When you enter any of the gateways to the soul you may so merge into God that there is complete and utter oneness and you suddenly find yourself in a state of contemplation. We can make ourselves open to this happening through contemplative prayer, where we progress through words and thoughts to a meditative state in which the mind neither wants nor is occupied with anything but the desire for God. All the hope, love, and trust we feel is bound up in our desire for this spiritual marriage of our true selves to God. To begin such contemplative prayer, you need to discard all observation, logic, analysis, words, and even your natural will. It is a total giving up of self. Make your praying God-filled by focusing only on the things of God and nothing of the ordinary world. Go so deep into yourself that all awareness and knowing disappears and you rest at last in 'the cloud of unknowing' where all you understand disappears and super-natural knowing is the state of your existence. Stay in this mystical realm where the divine and the human in you meet for as long as God allows. Such contemplation fixes you in the sublime things of eternity and heaven.

Even as human lovers call out to each other, so we call to our eternal Beloved. Our soul is caught up in holy desire. The mystical union with the Divine *is* possible. John Joseph Surin and St Teresa do not stand alone as witnesses. Thousands of mystics from every spiritual tradition and religion bear testimony to this manifestation of the perfected soul. When your heart calls out in prayer, 'Come, Lord! Come, Beloved!' you will be answered. God is there.

THE TENTH
GATEWAY

Creativity – the way of grounding the new vision

Everyone has his own gift from God, one this and
the next something different.

(1 Corinthians 7:7)

The work we do to earn a living and the activities of our
leisure time, from gardening and sewing to surfing and
mountain climbing, are expressions of our inherent
creativity, which springs from a deep urge to partici-
pate in the Creation around us and to make our contribution to
it. We want to celebrate life in so many different ways – swim with
dolphins, plant a seed, knit a sweater, paint a picture of flowers,
repair a bike for a ride in the country, because we are here to live
as fully as possible in this Creation of which we are so intimately
a part. The pleasure we get from exercising our creativity is a song
of praise for Creation itself. We realise that we each have unique
gifts and that our work (for gain or not) and our creative efforts
can contribute to keep our vision of life as the union of all things

– together in God.

For many people there are two obstacles that stand in front of the Gateway of Creativity and stop them from entering: we simply do not see how the work we do is creative and we do not believe everyone has unique gifts of creativity – especially ourselves.

The creativity of play

If people tell me they don't have a soul, I shrug and never argue because I know that somewhere in their heart a secret voice speaks to them of yearnings and things beyond the physical and mental. On the other hand, if people tell me they have no talents or personal gifts, then I really argue with them because they are denying the holy in themselves, which is always creative and unique. If they are made like that then they *must* have personal gifts. Discovering them is the greatest of creative adventures, so I always urge them on as I am urging you now.

The artistic impulse

Humanity has always contrived to provide itself with goods designed to make life more practical and comfortable. We also have an irresistible urge to enhance such objects with decorations – little touches that proclaim our individuality. While a great many of these decorations are practical and, indeed, many have been religious in nature, most serve no better cause than that of our artistic impulse. Crafts remain popular today in an age of plenty for this simple reason. But beyond expressing ourselves artistically with our knitting, cross-stitch, woodwork and renovating, there lurks a creativity that serves a spiritual purpose and takes us straight into the garden of the soul.

The work of our hands grounds us in a reality that we can see, touch and feel, and which can provide us with the knowedge of our own participation in Creation and that what we have done is uniquely an expression of our inner self. The work of our hands is like a direct line to earth and God. It disconnects us from concerns of the world and plugs us into inner concerns of the spirit. We are *creating* and this action joins us up to Creation itself. We have passed through the Gateway of Creativity.

With long working hours and all the responsibilities of daily life, our minds often become overactive. Our bodies may get a fast fix of exercise once a week – golf, squash, a run, gym class or some yoga. The problem is that all this being busy can disconnect us from the reality of our true inner nature and give us no time in which to meditate on the bigger issues and remember a greater vision of our life. Often it means we have no time to just *be*.

Many years ago I found myself alone with two young children and in a fast-paced and competitive job. The responsibilities piled up on me but I proudly handled it all with a schedule that left me no time to think. There was hardly ever a time to play. Millions of people handle such a schedule brilliantly – especially many women today. But I felt more and more that my life was an endless getting up in the morning and just doing it. Once in a while I would stop for a quick bit of prayer-time in the nearby church. Mostly I asked God to keep me going. This encouraged me to keep at my schedule. One autumn day I stopped outside the church, amazed by the colours of the trees. A little later, in the middle of praying, it suddenly came to me that I should be like the tree – changing, growing, and becoming, full of colour and surprise – because I too belonged to Creation. Did my busy schedule define me? Was my soul all one unchanging colour? On the way home I bought a needlepoint kit on impulse. Each evening when the kids were finally asleep, I sat down for half an hour and did some embroidery. I didn't tell anyone about it, not even the kids, because I thought they would make fun of me. But sitting still and pushing the needle in and out was like a meditation without words. It took me into my inner space where at long last I seemed to have peace and quiet. It made me feel real. Memories and dreams for the future flooded my mind. I felt at peace and closer to God. If something could be a revelation, I held it in my hands. It connected me back into myself. I still kept up my schedule because bills had to be paid and kids raised, but I kept going with the work of my hands. It brought me into different realities that were part of me too. In making something I could feel and touch and hold I was playing in the garden of my soul and it was fun. One day I got up enough courage to show my kids. They thought it was super. I started going to a night class in textiles, studied on holiday with a weaver and found I had a flair for the decorative. My stitching became a creative expression of me.

You too can discover something to make that will draw you from a too-busy world into your inner space. It does not matter what it is or how well you do it. What matters is that you are joining up with Creation through your own creativity. The actions of your hands make more than the things you see. They can take you into your inner space, bring you a sense of peace, and give you sanctuary from the frustrations, responsibilities and conflicts of the ordinary world. These little works create strong connections to the sacred.

If you do not already have a hobby or other leisure interest, start looking around for one. There are plenty of adult education classes and weekend courses that cover almost everything from carpentry and pottery to herb-growing. You do not need to begin with any special skills, because the idea is to express your inner self. This is the only standard you need for measuring your success. Think of something that other people create, that has always fascinated you, or something you have always wanted to make. Then find a course and sign up, or go to a shop and get the material and a manual on how to do it from the library. Keep it simple at first – knit some squares, build a shelf, put some new tiles around the bath – then go on to bigger projects as your confidence grows. Your family and friends are likely to be as encouraging as my kids were when I started stitching.

A lot of people worry too much about what is 'craft' and what is 'art' and this distinction gets in the way of their personal creativity. Some people feel that art has no end in mind except beauty or the perception of a new truth, while craft is about an end product which, while perhaps beautiful, serves a practical purpose. Yet without making any such distinction, we can equally admire the jewellery of Islam, the salt cellars of Cellini, and a painting by Édouard Manet. Any attempt at separating art from craft and declaring each 'different' in some way not only serves little purpose, as far as I am concerned, but has prevented many gifted people from undertaking the creating of things which satisfy their personal artistic impulse and so bring them closer to God through the discovery of their own uniqueness. Whether these things are embroidered cushions, watercolours, a workbench, or a pile of cupcakes is irrelevant – they can all be works of art because every one is a unique expression of that person, who is a unique expression of God. We are too eager in this age of the expert to decide what is 'good' and what is 'wrong' when such judgements are, after all, a matter of personal taste. And your personal taste is just as good as anybody else's and what you create is just as 'good' as the greatest painting. The reason for this is simply that when anyone is creative they are joining up with the whole process of Creation itself – they are evolving themselves, and this serves a holy purpose and connects them with the essence of living. In this there can be nothing but 'good'. This is the Gateway of Creativity, which is open to all of us.

Creativity and nature

Gardening is one of those creative activities that produces an enjoyable sensation of achievement. It is so many-sided that even if we all started off with similar rectangular plots, the end-products would be completely different.

The Well-Tempered Garden, Christopher Lloyd, (Collins, London, 1970)

Working outside in the garden or with plants in the house can keep you deeply in touch with nature. It is a way of connecting your inner self to the wider universe and feeling the oneness of life. Planting up a garden, weeding and tending it, or taking care of a few houseplants, draws our attention away from the concerns of our ego and into a focus on living things, and forces us to be creative about what we chose to cultivate and how we arrange the garden or pots. Planting seeds is always an act of hope, and the vitality of gardening – all that shovelling, digging, and pulling – are all actions that can bring a sense of inner peace. The satisfaction of a home-grown vegetable or bunch of flowers is tremendous. If you have not tried gardening, find a little patch of ground and plant it up. If you have no garden, buy a couple of houseplants or ask a friend for some cuttings. Grow and tend them. Think of them as growing in the garden of your soul. Water them as you would water yourself – with love, care and gentleness. Touch them as you would yourself – with tenderness and joy. Find in their growth and change a reflection of how you too grow and change. Make this creativity with your garden and plants a discovery of yourself. When the day comes – and well it might – that you *talk* to your roses or your African Violet – know then that you are indeed living in the sacred, for you have discovered that you and the roses and the African Violet are one and the same – unique creations that belong to each other in the spirit if not in appearance, because everything together creates the oneness of life.

Making work holy and creative

It can be hard to think of yourself as creative when you sit in an office all day pushing paper around, or work in a factory and never see the end product, or read and hear all the time about having a career when all you have is a job. Yet any work can be creative if we are willing to re-evaluate our attitude to it. Instead of thinking 'I do this only for the money' make it into a spiritual dynamic by affirming 'I am giving some of my life to this job, and since my life is sacred I will use my job to connect me to the spiritual things that matter to me.' Stop seeing work as a necessary evil that deserves as little effort as possible – just something you have to do until retirement – and look instead at how you could make it serve your spiritual life as well as your bank account. Entering the Gateway of Creativity is the result of thinking creatively; it doesn't depend on the kind of job you do.

Think of yourself as working in the garden of your soul – approach your work as a creative person. If it was a real garden you were creating, you would start with a vision and through focusing on that you would see the practical work needed to transform the tangled, weed-ridden ground into something that uplifts the spirit and makes you feel more alive. Three qualities are essential in transforming your work into a creative opportunity: respect, enthusiasm and commitment.

Respect

This means respecting yourself, your work, and your colleagues. Be prepared for your work. This means making sure your body, mind and spirit is ready for it. Make sure you get enough sleep. Try to leave any domestic or relationship worries outside the workplace so that you can focus your mind on the work you are doing. (This focusing will both ease your suffering and give your unconscious a chance to work on what is worrying you.) If your body and mind are ready for work, then you should feel quite peaceful about starting work. In this peace your spirit can feel free.

Are you always running late? The key word here is 'running' because it is symbolic of what is happening to your body, mind and spirit when you are late – they are running too fast and in the rush they cannot find balance. Not arriving at work on time is a bad start to the day because it fragments you: a part of you is always busy proving 'I don't want to *be* here!' Being on time will help you to live in the present moment and feel whole: it is like a clear space in which your creativity can unfold.

Approach your work with kindness to yourself. Are you organised so you do not have to hunt for things and get frustrated? Do you feel your appearance is the best you can do? Are you sitting or standing comfortably? When you get a rest break at work do you use it to find inner stillness and peace or do you chatter about the world's cares or rush about on errands that *must* get done? Taking a proper rest during work is meant to refresh your body, mind *and* spirit. It is a time to be kind to yourself

Having made space for your creativity at work, don't squash it back down by being judgemental. While we need to find our failings so we can accept and deal with them, self-criticism can be a very negative and uncreative process. There is no need to be constantly criticising yourself and your work. The key is to do your best. That is all any of us should ask of ourselves. So squash your self-criticism rather than your creativity and take notice each time you do the best job you can. Get into the habit of acknowledging your colleagues' successes as well – the more you encourage their creativity, the more supportive the work environment will be for all of you.

Enthusiasm

Turn up at work today with a new idea. It doesn't have to be grand or make a lot of money – just something no matter how small that could make a difference at work. Make a new commitment to your work – turn up today with the determination to do a better job than you did yesterday. New ideas and a new commitment will refresh your job.

If you are indifferent to the spiritual purpose of your work, you are being indifferent about yourself. This is not loving yourself. It puts a brake on your creativity. If nothing matters to you at work, ask yourself why not. There must be some nice people there; you are employed and not out searching for work; the job you do must bring some good to someone. Our indifference to work often stems from a desire to hide from the reality that our work is fully part of the scheme of our lives. If you are going to live a life of truth, why not start with your job. See its strengths and weaknesses and be indifferent to neither. Hunt around and find something positive in it that you can develop. Be creative about it.

You can apply your creativity to developing positive relationships at work. We probably spend more time with people at work than with anyone else. This gives us a great opportunity to practise loving. If you are a boss, try encouragement instead of criticism. If you are the lowest paid worker in the place, you can still be the most important when it comes to loving. Love makes you see the good in people and encourages you to treat them with as much consideration as you yourself would like to be given. This creates an interaction between you and your colleagues that enhances and makes the work itself more creative and rewarding. Let love become part of your work.

Commitment

No creative endeavour succeeds without commitment and determination. Don't expect instant results: you are working on a deep transformation of old habits, and you may have to deal with discouragement and other obstacles. Perseverance can be uncomfortable: it means steadfastly pursuing your aim, regardless of whether the way is smooth or rocky. Work can be like your spiritual life – lots of ups and downs. When a job is difficult don't decide you can't do it – keep trying; ask for some help; see it through. When your work is going well, count it as a blessing and celebrate by being happy. In this way the next time your work gets tough or boring or frustrating, remember your past successes. The process of perseverance fosters a sense of your work as a whole rather than being fragmented into separate tasks.

Being faithful to your work means that you insist sooner or later on work which you love. People who strive for this do not give up trying. They dare life to stop them from working at what they love – and earning a living from it. They are not just doing their work, they are making work part and parcel of their *being*. This is being faithful to your true self. You need to be creative to do this because you have to be actively engaged in finding out what kind of work you love and then going after it. Remember your soul doesn't care at all about what you are doing for a living, just what you are *being*.

> Whatever work you take up, do it whole-heartedly.
> Put all you have got into it. 'Whatever you do,'
> wrote the Apostle Paul, 'do it heartily, as to the Lord
> and not to men.'
>
> (Colossians 3:23)

Developing your creativity at work in this way will ensure you feel a sense of dignity, no matter how important or modest your work is in the eyes of the world; a self-discipline that keeps your body, mind and spirit in balance in your everyday life; and the delight a sense of unity between all parts of your life can bring to all you do. To have dignity, to be disciplined and to be delighted reflect a changed attitude to your life and are springboards to belief in yourself. This belief is central to your creativity and grounds you in a new vision of reality whether you are at work or play.

Five keys to creativity at work

1. Look for the positive in the job you do. Be creative about it. Say to yourself: 'There must be *something* interesting about this job.' Then hunt for it, no matter how small and hidden it may at first appear. Make it big. Make it positive.

2. Take God to work by practising sacred virtues like love and faithfulness. First practise them with regard to yourself and your real feelings, then with your colleagues. Remember that you can always talk to God wherever you are and whatever you are doing. These little conversations will remind you that you are as spiritual at work as anywhere else.

3. If you feel you are not in a job that makes your heart glad, go for one that does. Fear not and believe in yourself. Pray for it. Remember that when you love yourself you will discover what makes your heart glad. That will help you to find the right job.

4. Do not overwork and leave no time for play. A dulled and fatigued body and mind casts a shadow on the soul. Many people work too hard today either at their job or at home. If you are always too busy, you are likely to be too busy to pay much attention to God. This means you are neglecting your inner space. Take time for the sanctuary of the garden of your soul. Make certain that you leave time to go there often. Keep work and play in balance with the things of God.

5. The problem of plenty is that it can cost us spiritually. More is not always better. Learn to be creative with what you already earn and possess. Remember to want eternal things, not just worldly ones. These priceless treasures you earn by working in the garden of your soul.

The need for patience

We live in a world in which the goal is immediacy. We do not expect to be kept waiting – fast checkouts, fast food, fast service. We have learned not to be patient.

Being impatient sticks our ego on to centre stage: we think ourselves important. It pushes us into all sorts of fevered activity, as if there were no tomorrow, as if the world would stop if we dared not to finish a chore, were late for work, forgot to buy something at the shops or missed a telephone call or voice mail or sales opportunity. In this way impatience creates in us anxieties, self-importance, and a lack of inner calm. We feel *driven*. This is a real block to knowing anything about your true feelings, including your creativity – you are simply too busy to have any insights.

Being easily bored is a form of impatience. Our attention span shortens until we must constantly seek new distractions and sensations. It is as if doing the same thing for too long would diminish us, make us somehow less *individual*. This means you think what you do defines who you are. This is not a spiritual proposition. On the contrary, we occasionally need to be like a monk and 'stay in our cell' – that is to remain in a situation and control our impatience because it is based on desires for the fleeting things of the world. We need to learn to be contented from time to time with the same routine, the same kind of food, the same faces, the same occupations, and even with the same slow service.

This practise of patience can give you valuable inner space time and quiet you down. Such moments can mean an extra helping of that inner solitude that refreshes the spirit. You can practise patience for such a spiritual purpose just as well as the monk in his cell because patience and its gift of solitude live within us. That interior place is your own spiritual cell, which is called the soul; and time has no measure there so why hurry? Here patience becomes spiritual wisdom and is called by another name: *silent courage*. So the monk, and all who would strive to live a sacred life, must forgo impatience which disturbs the soul, stirs up all manner of worldly desires, and denies the timelessness of our spiritual dimension. If you get impatience under control, you can begin to think about your true feelings and discover the resources of your creativity.

Many things need to be nurtured by patience. Think of the flower seeds you sow or spring bulbs slowly inching their way into the light. Think of a child putting together a jigsaw puzzle for the first time or beginning to read. You need patience not just with others but for yourself. Patience is a soothing salve for the mind and gives your heart time to open. When you begin creative work of the hands or go on a course, do not become impatient with your work or bored because you don't seem to understand and get something correct first off – or even the hundredth time. Keep your heart open, because this keeps your creativity flourishing. Count to ten, close your eyes and say a prayer for patience, use some personal discipline, and try again. The reasons you are there are spiritual ones. Keep going by practising patience.

Become an artist of life

The real answers about your true self can only be given by your inner voice. What the Gateway of Creativity in all its forms does is to stimulate your awareness of your uniqueness through the discovery and use of your own gifts. This helps keep you connected to a new vision of your life. But just as the flowers in your garden may have beauty and colour but no scent, so a person who knows wise things but does not practise them lives without truth. So we need to make our creativity part of our spiritual life every day. Whether it is used at work or in play, creativity expresses our gifts. These reflect our true selves and give us cause to reflect. Maybe you can't paint pictures or make things or dig a garden, but you can still be an artist. Here is how: take up your life like clay. Feel it. Give it edges, lightness, colour, shape, and vision. Be an artist of your own life. This is the grandest creativity of all.

THE WISE TRAVELLER

When we have passed through a gateway into the garden of the soul, we soon realise that if we want a spiritual life then we must unify our life. Thomas Merton believed that a life is either all spiritual or not spiritual at all, because no one can serve two masters at the same time. You can serve either the passing illusions and desires of the world, which so often bring suffering, or you can serve the purposes of a spiritual life in which you seek to discover and free your true self. Our lives are always shaped by the end we live for, and in time we become the image of what we desire. The wise traveller learns that a yearning for the holy brings eternal values and union with Creation. We become the image of God. Our vision has gone beyond what the eye can see and the ear hear, to what the soul proclaims.

When we live a life in which our experience and knowledge is used to enrich and ease our way to wholeness, we can be said to have wisdom. The source of this wisdom is our personal integrity. A person with integrity is someone who is honest with themselves and other people, and someone who is whole and true to themselves. Arriving at this deep understanding of yourself entails a great pilgrimage to the heart of your personal truth. This is the journey of the spirit, and when you arrive in the garden of your

soul you will be wise with the things of God and wary of the ways
of humanity.

All this transforms not just the way you live but your insights
into your true self. Here wisdom takes root. A person who does not
live in this manner becomes a spiritual drifter – an inauthentic
person who is never whole. They are so excited by the new, by the
ever-changing view of possibilities in the distance, that they never
experience the present. Their spiritual dabbling brings no transformation of self. It is as if such people are hunters who carry no
weapons and haven't actually decided what it is they're hunting.
St Paul summed them up this way: 'Always seeking learning and
never able to come to the knowledge of the truth.' (2 Timothy 3:7).
The wise traveller knows that what must prevail if we are to use
our experience and knowledge to model and transform our lives is
much more than just an acceptance of ourselves and the basic
conditions of our humanity. We must commit ourselves to a way
of living that reflects a spiritual ultimatum, and this disposes of
much of our confusion. Whatever the truths to which we commit
ourselves, our commitment gives to them a horizon beyond which
we may sense a kind of eternal certainty. It brings us a life of unity
rather than one in which we are fragmented and aimless, adrift on
a sea of illusions and desires, and a prisoner of our senses. In living a life of such personal moral commitment we live a sacred life
where what is important transcends human values and mirrors
eternal ones of love, compassion, and hope.

Certainty and compassion

The essence of living is change, and change is the mother of all
uncertainty. The kind of certainty that many want is earthly and
is the foundation of bigots. It says 'here is the real truth' and it is
always false. Compassion, on the other hand, is what the wise
traveller tries to find, for compassion makes us think we might just
be wrong. It brings a true social sense because it is selfless love.

Compassion means we understand that the *I* does not know, cannot produce answers to the spiritual yearning of others, does not hold them in any kind of bondage, nor have the capacity to 'save' them. Compassion begets kindness. It raises up saints and fosters love. It helps us to leave our desire for certainty with God and to await his pleasure. This strengthens us with hope for the future and stills our fear of the as-yet-unknown changes in our lives. Compassion is the vehicle of wisdom for every wise traveller.

The sevenfold perfection of the heart

The wise traveller manifests their love for the holy in their daily life. The following seven aspects of spiritual perfection, based on the mystical revelations of Mechthild of Magdeburg, can help you to do this if you call them to mind frequently and use them as ways to open your heart. In spite of how contrary they may be to the current views of society, none of these virtues diminish our dignity or lessen our identity. They are a good antidote to any belief we may have in the importance of ourselves.

1. To find contentment in solitude. If you know yourself you will have a lifelong companion. The wise traveller is never lonely.
2. To enjoy stillness of the soul. Peace comes from within you. It is the gift of wholeness. The wise traveller is always at peace.
3. To be thankful to be esteemed. To accept love is to accept yourself. The wise traveller practises self-love.
4. Not to care about your status in society. If you do not know your own worth, you do not know yourself. The wise traveller knows there is nothing higher than to be one with God.
5. To rejoice in being one of many. When you are aware of belonging to all Creation, your vision includes the whole

universe. The wise traveller rejoices in all life.

6. To be faithful in the midst of falseness. To remain loyal to your beliefs in the face of the passing attractions of the world is to desire truth. The wise traveller defends the freedom of the soul.

7. To love without sorrow of the heart. To love without regret is to love without possessing so you remain happy in what you have given, not what you have received. The wise traveller makes love a gift without strings.

We are always imperfect in our use of the perfection of life. We may regret our inadequacy, but we need to remember that we are still immensely precious to God. Our faith in God's love gives us the grace to continue to strive in the spiritual life and to reckon our success to be as much in the pilgrimage as the arrival.

No one can give us the final answers to our spirituality, for it is intimately connected with who we are. Wisdom always gives the same advice if we want to live a sacred life and find God: know thyself. This is the paramount task of our life. The fruit of our labour is the discovery of our true self, and there we find God waiting. This journey transcends all human events and creations and gives profound meaning to our lives. Until we make this journey we remain in exile from the deepest meanings of our own being because these are not obtained by reason but by faith.

The four maxims
of a sacred life

What matters then is not what can be seen – the things of this
world which decay and pass away and never fill our soul with lasting joy. What matters is what is unseen: the love in our lives, the
happiness we create in others, the bliss of knowing our children
are safe, the kindness of a stranger, the pleasure of a friend's
companionship. These are the unseen but eternal things we
should pursue every day. To live this way is to throw open all the
gateways to the soul and to use them as spiritual tools in cultivating a sacred life. We can know the enlightenment of the Buddha
for what it is. In holding up such a mirror of our being, we will see
the Christ.

These four maxims will guide you in each step of the way:

1. Submit your heart completely to the will of God so that
   you may become your true self.
2. Resolve to overcome all the difficulties you encounter in
   seeking a spiritual life.
3. Remember that God purifies you from time to time with
   trials and difficulties and you should not be discouraged by
   these but remain hopeful.
4. Recognise that you need God's help in every moment of
   your life as much for the small as for the grand, because
   your passing desires and the world continuously wage war
   on your soul.

Wherever you are at this moment, and whatever your successes or
failures, weaknesses or strengths, fame or fortune, the garden of
your soul awaits you. Journey there so that you may always live a
life that includes opening your heart to the mystery of yourself. To
live a sacred life is to sanctify life. You cannot give greater honour
to your life than this ideal of love.

Further Reading

In quoting from the Bible, I have used the following editions: The New Jerusalem Bible (Darton, Longman & Todd, London, 1990), The Good News Bible (The Bible Society / HarperCollins, London, 1994) and The New King James Version (Thomas Nelson, USA, 1982). All quotations from the psalms are from *The Psalms*, ed. Joseph Gelineau (Fount Paperbacks, London, 1963).

The following are a few books which will help you in your meditations and in living a sacred life.

General

In Search of Nature, Edward O. Wilson (Island Press, Washington DC, 1996)

Kinship with the Animals, ed. Michael Tobias and K. Solisti-Mattelon (Beyond Worlds Publishing, USA, 1998)

The Phenomenon of Man, Pierre Teilhard de Chardin (Fount Paperbacks, London, 1983)

Science and the Soul, Angela Tilby (SPCK, London, 1992)

The Varieties of Religious Experience, William James (Longmans, Green & Co., London, 1929)

Buddhism

Ancient Wisdom, Modern World, The Dalai Lama (Little, Brown, 1999)

The Buddha and His Religion, J. Bartélmy Saint-Hilaire (Tiger Books, Middlesex, 1998)

Cittaviveka: Teachings from the silent mind, Ven. Ajahn Sumedho (Amaravati Buddhist Centre, Hertfordshire, 1987)

Christianity

An Anthology of Mysticism, ed. Paul de Jaegher (Burns & Oates, London, 1977)

Confessions of St Augustine, trans. R. S. Pine-Coffin (Penguin, London, 1961)

The Interior Castle, Teresa of Avila (Paulist Press, New York, 1981)

Interior Prayer: Carthusian novice conferences (Darton, Longman & Todd, London, 1996)

Introducing the New Testament, John Drane (Lion Books, Oxford, 1986)

Introducing the Old Testament, John Draine, (Lion Books, Oxford, 1987)

A Life-giving Way: A commentary on the Rule of St Benedict, Esther de Waal (Geoffrey Chapman, 1995)

Meister Eckhart: The Essential Sermons, trans. Edmund Colledge (Paulist Press, New York, 1981)

The Mysticism of the Cloud of Unknowing, William Johnston, (Anthony

Clarke, Hertfordshire, 1978)

New Seeds of Contemplation, Thomas Merton (New Directions, 1972)

The Practice of the Presence of God, Brother Lawrence (Mowbray, London, 1980)

The Revelations of Mechtild of Magdeburg, Lucy Menzies (Longmans, Green & Co., London, 1953)

A Thirst for God: Daily readings with St Francis de Sales (Darton, Longman & Todd, London, 1985)

Thoughts in Solitude, Thomas Merton (Burns & Oates, London, 1975)

Hinduism

Bhagavad-Gita: Chapters 1–6, Maharishi Mahesh Yogi (Penguin, London, 1969)

A Short Introduction to Hinduism, Klaus K. Klostermaier (Oneworld, Oxford, 1998)

Islam

The Essential Rumi, trans. Coleman Barks (Harper San Francisco, 1995)

Essential Sufism, ed. James Fadiman and Robert Frager (Harper San Francisco, 1997)

The Koran, trans. N. J. Dawood (Allen Lane, London, 1978)

Muhammad: A short biography, Martin Forward (Oneworld, Oxford, 1998)

The Mystics of Islam, Reynold A. Nicholson (Arkana, London, 1989)

A Short Introduction to Islamic Philosophy, Theology and Mysticism, Majid Fakhry (Oneworld, Oxford, 1998)

Understanding the Qur'an: Themes and style, Muhammad Abdel Haleem (I. B. Tauris, London, 1999)

Judaism

Kabbalah: The way of the Jewish mystic, Perle Epstein (Shambhala, London, 1988)

Shamanism

The Book of the Hopi, Frank Walters (Penguin, London, 1963)

Myths, Dreams and Mysteries, Mircea Eliade (Collins, London, 1977)

Native American Spirituality, Dennis Renault and Timothy Freke (Thorsons, London, 1996)

The Way of the Shaman, Michael Harner (HarperCollins, New York, 1990)

Zen

The Golden Age of Zen, John C. H. Wu (Image Books, Doubleday, New York, 1996)